Saints' N[...] for Your Baby

Fiona MacMath

Marshall Pickering
An Imprint of HarperCollins*Publishers*

Marshall Pickering is an Imprint of
HarperCollins*Religious*
Part of HarperCollins*Publishers*
77–85 Fulham Palace Road
London W6 8JB

First published in Great Britain
in 1997 by Marshall Pickering

3 5 7 9 10 8 6 4 2

Copyright © 1997 Fiona MacMath

Fiona MacMath asserts the moral right to be
identified as the author of this work

A catalogue record for this book is
available from the British Library

0 551 030259

Printed and bound in Great Britain by
Caledonian International Book Manufacturing Ltd, Glasgow

Dedicated to
Elizabeth Anne Vinten Pinner

Introduction

Our babies come into the world as surprise parcels, each with a unique bundle of characteristics. We have to wait to see them gradually unfold but cannot wait until then, though, to give them names; so we choose a name in the hope that they will grow into it and like it. We choose names because they sound well, because they belong to someone we love or because they mean something important to us.

For centuries, people have bestowed a saint's name on their baby in the hope that their child will grow up like its namesake – even though many of the saints were notoriously difficult to live with! The saints are also believed to offer a range of services to their protégés: protection, of course, help for specific problems, such as the rigours of travelling and help for special talents, like music or resourcefulness. For example, a child called Clare – named after St Francis's prayerful companion – might be able to draw on the single-mindedness, charity and kindness of her namesake. More prosaically, she is the patron saint of television: her name means 'light'. (Ironically, she is also invoked to help sore eyes.)

Some ideas for a future career, perhaps? St George might point to a profession in the armed forces. St

Cecilia could give your budding musician an unfair advantage over everyone else. St Anne might have a child dedicated to her if she had helped with a difficult birth; and St Giles is traditionally the special saint of anyone born with a handicap of some sort.

To bear the name of a saint certainly means having something to live up to – or even to live down. It would be a very unkind parent who christened their child Ethelburga or Willibald. But to have a 'heavenly' godmother or godfather is to be part of the tradition of the Church, to have a name which is familiar throughout the Christian world. It is to have a star to follow.

How, then, do you choose a saint's name for your baby? In medieval times, people seem to have been led more by devotion to certain popular saints than conventional ideas about what girls or boys should be called – many girls were christened in honour of male saints, with what we would think of nowadays as exclusively boys' names. Since the Church's calendar remembers several saints on any given day in the year, babies were often christened hastily by a priest after the saint's feast day on which they were born. Since some Christians (particularly Roman Catholics and Orthodox) celebrate a person's 'name day' even more splendidly than his or her birthday, it might be an advantage to choose a saint whose feast day is a good way off from the actual birthday – and thus have two celebrations every year.

If you are not familiar with the way Christians have venerated the saints, you may be rather surprised by what you read. Some appear to be mythological, some seem to be characters in legends. Others seem to have been canonized simply because they died in a horrible way or because they had a dubious reputation for weird phenomena like levitation or miraculous healing. The veneration of so many women for choosing death rather than marriage is at odds with our own century's veneration of sexual fulfilment and it may now seem rather pointless. But it is faith and love that matter, and no one without these – however spiritually powerful or gruesomely killed – can be called a saint.

Where there is little information available about a particular saint, perhaps the faith and love of the people who have been inspired by him or her is of the most importance. It is a kind of devotion to God through a human character who is more recognizably like ourselves or closer to our own culture than Jesus is – and He does not despise our need to see Him in human form.

This book will give you an idea of some traditional saints' names which are popular today, with something about their first owners – their characters, their special interests and their dates, where they are known. It may surprise you to see how many variations there are on some names. For instance, Ewan, Siobhan, Joan, Janine, Owen and Jack are all variations on the name of John. Each entry has variations usually associated with boys, and those that tend to belong to girls, although these distinctions have never been hard and fast. At the end of the book, there is a calendar of saints, which contains a name for every day of the year. The calendars of Christian churches differ, and are changed slightly from time to time, so you may like to do further research yourself if you have a favourite saint.

A

St Adrian

Meaning: 'from Adria', a port on the Adriatic Sea.

Variation: Adrien

Female variations: Adrianne, Adrienne

This name became widely known in England in the twelfth century, when Nicholas Breakespear took it on becoming the first and only English pope – Adrian IV. It was actually St Adrian III, however, who was canonized, although no one knows much about his life. An earlier Adrian, and his companion Eubulus, were martyred in Caesarea in 309 for visiting the Christians in prison there, and there was a St Adrian martyred by the Danes on one of their raids on the Scottish coasts in the ninth century. Another St Adrian was an African who became the Abbot of Canterbury, where he died peacefully in 710.

The most well-known St Adrian, married to St Natalia, was also martyred, in 304, for looking after persecuted Christians. He was a Roman soldier in Nicomedia who was so impressed by his Christian prisoners that he joined them. His wife encouraged him in his quest for martyrdom, and is herself venerated as a martyr, although she fled to Agyropolis after his execution, where she died of natural causes.

Feast day: 8 September.

Symbols: armour; a hammer and anvil; a key; a wheel.

Patron: of arms dealers, butchers and prison officers.

St Alice

Meaning: from Old German, 'nobility'.

Female variations: Alison, Alicia, Alyssa, Alisa, Adelaide, Aleydis, Alys

St Alice was a twelfth-century Cistercian nun from Brussels, who contracted leprosy. It was an immense tragedy for her because she had to accept solitary confinement, and was unable to drink Communion wine from the chalice. Her life and faith, sustained by visions, was described by a member of her community and Alice was canonized for her patience in suffering.

Feast day: 15 June.

St Agnes

Meaning: **from the Greek, 'pure'.**

Female variations: Agneta, Annis, Ines, Inez, Nessle, Nesta, Senga

St Agnes (whose name sounds like the Latin *agnus* or 'lamb') was reputedly the daughter of a wealthy Christian Roman family during the reign of the Emperor Diocletian (284–305), when Christians were savagely persecuted. She is remembered for her determination to remain a virgin, in spite of all the entreaties and threats of Eutropius, the son of a Roman governor, who had fallen in love with her. She was humiliated and threatened with rape by Eutropius, who – legend has it – was immediately struck blind, and then miraculously cured by Agnes herself. Eventually, she was sentenced to be burnt at the stake, but the fire seemed more inclined to burn the spectators than her, so she was eventually stabbed to death in 304 or 305. She was only 13 years old. She is one of the few women saints who are mentioned in the liturgy of the Roman Catholic Mass.

'To play the Agnes' is a French expression to describe a young girl who is completely innocent of any idea of love, and Molière includes her as a character in his play, *L'ecole des Femmes*. In Britain, however, St Agnes' Eve was the time when a young girl might be granted a vision of her future husband if she fasted and observed certain rituals before going to bed. Aubrey's *Miscellany* suggests:

> *Upon St Agnes' night, you take a row of pins and pull out every one, one after another. Saying a paternoster, stick a pin in your sleeve, and you will dream of him or her you shall marry.*

Alternatively, you could fast all day and then eat an egg with salt just before going to bed, or sit up late at your mirror in the hope of catching a glimpse of his face appearing over your shoulder…

Feast day: 21 January.

Symbols: a lamb; a dove holding a ring; a sword.

Patron: of young girls, virgins and Girl Guides.

St Albert

Meaning: **from Old German, 'noble bright'.**

Variations: Aubert, Bertie, Bert

Female variation: Alberta

The name Albert has fallen out of favour after its immense popularity with the Victorians – perhaps it is due for a revival. There are at least seven saints who bear the name, but two are particularly inspiring for us today.

The first, Albert the Great, a German, became one of the most advanced scientists of his age (the thirteenth century). He resigned his bishopric in Regensburg and devoted himself to writing books on logic and mathematics, astronomy and geography, physics and chemisty, the natural sciences and philosophy, as well as theology and ethics. It was under his influence that Thomas Aquinas was encouraged to develop his own systematic theology based on scientific methods.

Feast day: 15 November.

Patron: of all those involved in scientific and medical research.

Another St Albert, Albert Chmielkowski, was a Polish painter who lost a leg in an uprising against the Russians in 1863, when he was only 18 years old. He later joined the Third Order of the Franciscans (for lay men and women), and made his studio into a shelter for the poor and homeless, before becoming a tramp himself; he died in a hospice in Cracow on Christmas Day, 1916. He might be the inspiration for the 'Crisis at Christmas movement', now simply called 'Crisis' – an organization which helps the destitute all year round.

Feast day: 25 December.

St Alexander

Meaning: **from the Greek, 'defender of men'.**

Variations: Alec, Alex, Alastair, Alisdair, Alexis, Sandy, Sacha

Female variations: Alex, Alexis, Alexei, Alessandra, Sandy, Sandie, Sandra, Alla, Zandra, Sasha

St Alexander of the Sleepless Ones may be an unwelcome but apt name for a baby. This Alexander was a fifth-century army officer in Constantinople. He was prompted to resign his commission and become a monk by the words of Jesus: 'If thou wilt be perfect, go and sell that thou hast, and give to the poor, and thou shalt have treasure in heaven; and come, follow me' (Matthew 19:21). Stories about his holiness and miracle-working were written down by one of his monks in Greek. The 'sleepless ones' were 300 monks who settled with him near Constantinople. Alexander divided them into six choirs to sing the divine office in turn – day and night – so that they could be praising God ceaselessly, and watching faithfully for the return of Christ.

Feast day: 15 January or 23 February.

St Andrew

Meaning: **from the Greek, 'manly'.**

Variations: Andrea, Anders, Andy, Drew, André

Female variations: Andrea, Andrée

There have been many Andrews who have been canonized or beatified but all take their name, of course, from the first disciple of Jesus. Andrew was a fisherman who was called from his nets to become 'a fisher of men', bringing with him Peter, his brother. Along with Peter and John, Andrew became one of Jesus' closest disciples. Like most of the apostles, the legends about his life after the Crucifixion are very colourful and most improbable. It is thought, however, that he also was crucified, on an X-shaped cross, in Patras, Achaia (Greece).

According to legend, Saints Rule and Theneva later took Andrew's bones to Scotland, obeying the voice of an angel which told them to take his relics 'to the ends of the earth'. Apparently, this revived Andrew; all three built St Andrew's church, and he became Scotland's patron saint, as well as the patron of Russia and Greece.

Feast day: 30 November.

Symbols: an X-shaped cross; two fishes; a fish hook; fishing nets.

Patron: of fishermen, sailors, spinsters and those with gout.

St Angel

Meaning: from the Greek, 'messenger'.

Variation: Angelo

The name 'Angel' is rare in English-speaking countries, despite Thomas Hardy's use of it in his novel *Tess of the D'Urbevilles*. Yet it is common in Italy where several Angelos were beatified, and where St Angelo, a Sicilian Carmelite, was murdered in 1220.

Feast day: 5 May.

Symbols: red and white roses; lilies; three crowns; a book.

St Angela

Female variations: Angelica, Angelina, Angeline

Much more common than Angel is its female form, Angela. The Blessed Angela of Foligno was a woman of prayer and mysticism. She was an ordinary thirteenth-century Italian wife and mother until she underwent a sudden conversion and joined the Third Order of the Franciscans. This was an order of 'Tertiaries' – men and women who could not, for various reasons, go into a monastery, but who wished to live by the monastic rules of poverty, chastity and obedience in the world. After her husband died, she was able to give away her wealth and attracted a large number of other people to the Third Order, who were impressed by her depth of prayer. Her confessor wrote down her account of some of her mystical experiences, and she is remembered on the 28 February.

St Angela Merici was the foundress of the Ursuline order (named after St Ursula) – the first teaching order for women. She was born in Italy in 1474 and orphaned at 15. She became a Franciscan tertiary, and became increasingly aware of the poverty of her native town, Desenzano. Determined to do something to help, she began to teach the poorest children, helped by some other women tertiaries. This practice later developed into a community of women who shared a common rule of life and devoted themselves to teaching and caring for young women and children. It was not an easy vocation – women were expected to live in enclosed communities, in traditional Orders, wear habits and take their inspiration from men. Eventually, after her death, Angela's women were forced to conform to a more traditional Order. Nevertheless, her vision was important for the development of nursing, education and independence of Christian women.

Feast day: 27 January.

Patron: of universities and women.

St Anne

Meaning: **from the Hebrew, 'graceful'.**

Female variations: Anna, Anette, Anya, Annie, Hannah, Nan, Nana, Nancy, Nita

It might be said that if St Anne had not existed, Christianity would have had to invent her – so important are grandmothers in the natural order of life. St Anne was the grandmother of Jesus, at least according to the apocryphal *Protoevangelion of St James*. Although nothing certain is known about her life, she can be seen – together with Mary and Jesus – in numerous Renaissance paintings. The account of Anna and her husband Joachim's miraculous conception of Mary may be strongly related to the Hebrew story of Hannah's conception of Samuel; in the same way, Mary's song – the Magnificat – echoes Hannah's song of triumphant joy. The mystery of Mary's birth has become known and honoured by many Christians, especially Roman Catholics, as the 'Immaculate Conception'.

Feast day: 26 July.

Symbols: an angel; a flowering rod; a crown; a nest of young birds; Mary in a cradle.

Patron: of housewives and grandmothers, pregnant women, cabinet makers and Canada.

St Anthony

Meaning: possibly 'beyond price' (Latin – one of the patrician Roman families)

Variations: Anton, Antoine, Tony

Female variations: Antonia, Antoinette, Antonella, Netta, Nettie, Netty, Toni, Tonia, Tonie, Tony

There are two famous St Anthonys in the Church. The first, Anthony the Great, is often known as the 'father of monasticism', for it was he who gathered together many of the fourth-century hermits who had fled from worldly distractions into the desert. These first Desert Fathers were famous for their lives of pathological self-denial and prayer; St Athanasius' biography of Anthony, however, shows him to have been a wise and moderate man, even though he suffered terrifying temptations through visions. He is supposed to have died around 365 at the age of 105. The smallest pig in a litter and the smallest bell in a carillon are often called the 'tantony', thus they have become his symbols: the little pig for the mortal flesh he conquered, and the bell as the traditional symbol of hermits.

Feast day: 17 January.

Symbols: a pig; a goat; two lions; a Tau cross (T); a bell.

Patron: of basket and brush makers (the first occupation of the Desert Fathers), butchers, grave diggers and pigs; he is often invoked by eczema sufferers.

The second very well-loved St Anthony was Portuguese (1195–1231), a Franciscan monk born in Lisbon, although he is known as St Anthony of Padua where he is buried. His reputation for finding lost things is based on a story that a novice once 'borrowed' his prayer book; Anthony prayed for its recovery and the novice returned it after finding himself tormented by a terrible vision.

Anthony's life's work was not finding lost objects, but rather being 'the hammer of the heretics' – having been commissioned in a vision by Francis himself to go and preach, mainly in Italy and France. A tale is told that Anthony shamed the people of Rimini, who would not listen to him, by preaching to the fish in the river, causing them to stand on their tails and listen devoutly. Although he is often pictured as a gentle man, with a Christ-child and lily, Anthony should not be thought of as anyone but a man of great intelligence and energy, full of the Franciscan passion for helping the poor.

Feast day: 13 June.

Symbols: the Christ-child on a book; lilies; fishes; a chest with a heart.

Patron: of the poor, unmarried women and Portugal; also invoked for good harvests and by those looking for lost property.

St Audrey

Meaning: **from Old English, 'noble strength'.**

Female variation: Etheldreda

The word 'tawdry' developed as a name for the sort of gaudy rubbish sold at the great St Audrey's Fair at Ely, Cambridgeshire, on her feast day, and Shakespeare uses 'Audrey' as the name of his irrepressibly lumpen country wench in *As You Like It*. The original Audrey, however, was the beautiful and determined princess Etheldreda; she seems to have lived up to her name. She was born in a village outside Newmarket in about 630 and took a vow of celibacy which she upheld, even when – for reasons of state – she was twice married. The Bishop, St Wilfrid, supported her resolution, and she eventually founded the Abbey of Ely, one of the great double monasteries of the period, in 672. It was famous for its austerity and prayer under her rule, which lasted until 679, when she died of a tumour on her neck.

Feast day: 23 June (or 17 October in the *Book of Common Prayer*).

Symbols: a sunflower; an open money chest.

Patron: of those with diseases of the throat and neck, and of Ely.

B

St Barbara

Meaning: **from the Greek, 'a foreigner'.**

Female variations: Bab, Babette, Barbie, Varina

No one knows if, when or where Barbara really existed. The legend – a seventh-century romance – tells of a beautiful girl who was imprisoned in a tower by her own father, Dioscurus, in order to keep men – especially Christian men – away. But a doctor managed to get into the tower to teach her about the Christian faith, which she immediately accepted – much to her father's fury. Although Barbara survived the torture of the authorities, her father cut off her head, upon which he was struck by lightning and completely incinerated. Whether true or simply a legend, Barbara became a well-loved patron, particularly by those who worked with explosives or those in need of help during thunderstorms.

Feast day: 4 December.

Symbols: a chalice; a host and paten (Communion plate); a tower with three windows; a tower and palm leaf; peacock feather; torches; a sword.

Patron: of architects (because she added a third window to her tower, in honour of the Trinity), gunsmiths, miners, firefighters, pyrotechnists and sailors.

St Barnabas

Meaning: **from the Hebrew, 'son of consolation'.**

Variations: Barnaby, Barney

Although Barnabas was not one of the Twelve, he is called an 'apostle' – that is, 'one who is sent'. Barnabas worked tirelessly to bring the Gospel to the people of the Roman Empire; indeed, his first mission was to be a companion to the newly-converted Paul (also called an apostle) when many Christians in Jerusalem could only remember him as the raging persecutor, Saul, who witnessed the stoning of St Stephen. We know from Acts that Barnabas was a Cypriot Jew, 'a good man, full of the Holy Ghost and of faith'. He accompanied Paul on his first missionary journey and is honoured as the founder of the Church on Cyprus.

Barnabas was also the cousin of John Mark, the young man who may have written the first Gospel. John Mark started out on the mission with them but disgraced himself – in Paul's eyes, at least – by wearying of the dangers. Barnabas, to his everlasting credit, took the part of the younger man and went back with him, although later he managed to reconcile the two. The Bible does not tell us what became of Barnabas, although tradition says that he was martyred at Salamis, Greece. Since Barnabas' feast day is the 11 June (the old style Midsummer Day), he has become the patron saint of haymakers and harvesters, as well as of Cyprus.

Feast day: 11 June.

Symbols: a dalmatic (the special vestment worn by a deacon at Communion); three stones; a hatchet.

Patron: of harvesters and Cyprus.

St Bartholomew

Meaning: **'son of Tolmai'; from the Hebrew, 'son of a farmer'.**

Variations: Bart, Bartelmy, Tolly

Female variation: Bartholomea

The original Bartholomew was one of the 12 disciples, possibly even the Nathaniel mentioned in John's Gospel, but nothing definite is known about him. It is said that he took the Gospel to Armenia where he was martyred by being flayed alive. His name was given to several Italian saints, and also Bartholomew of Farne, a Yorkshireman. This Bartholomew was ordained in Norway, but returned to Britain and spent 42 years on

Farne until his death in 1193. His feast day is on 24 June. It is also worth mentioning the remarkable Italian nun, Bartholomea Capitanio, who founded the Sisters of Charity of Lovere in Lombardy, with Vincentia Gerosa. Bartholomea wrote several books on the spiritual life, and is still remembered as a strong and unselfish woman. She died at the age of 26. Her feast day is on 26 July.

Feast day: 24 August.

Symbols: a scimitar; three knives; the devil under his feet; St Matthew's Gospel.

Patron: of Armenia, cheese merchants, and tanners.

St Benedict

Meaning: **from the Latin, 'blessed'.**

Variations: Ben, Bendix, Benedick, Benet, Bennett, Benito, Bennie, Benny

Female variations: Benedicta, Benita, Bennie, Benny, Binnie

As St Anthony the Great is known as the 'father of monasticism' as a whole, St Benedict (480–c.550) is the father of that particular form we know so well in the West – the Benedictine Rule, still hugely influential in the Church today. Monks and nuns live, work and pray in monastic houses, while keeping alive the tradition of learning, the arts and hospitality. Benedict was an Italian, born to aristocratic parents, and had a twin sister who was also canonized as St Scholastica. His own monastery was founded at Monte Cassino in 547. Apart from his wisdom and moderation, Benedict was also known as a great healer and one through whom God would raise the dead.

Feast day: 11 July.

Symbols: a ball of fire, a raven and a pitcher; briars and roses; a broken cup with a serpent on a book; a convent on a mountain.

Patron: of architects, farm workers, monks and Europe.

St Bernard

Meaning: from Old German, 'strong as a bear'.

Variations: Barnard, Barnet, Barney, Bern, Bernhard, Bernie, Berny

Most people think of those splendid, long-haired mountain rescue dogs when they think of St Bernard, and these were named after St Bernard of Montjoux (996–1081); his feast day is on 28 May and he is – predictably enough – patron saint of skiers and mountaineers. He was known for his pastoral care of the people of the Alpine valleys of Aosta, Italy, and he set up two hospices for travellers on the passes which now bear his name. The more ecclesiastically distinguished St Bernard of Clairvaux was born about 10 years afterwards, and became a founder of 68 Cistercian monasteries, as well as playing a part in politics and Church councils. He wrote so beautifully that he became known as 'Doctor Mellifluous' or 'the honey-sweet Doctor'.

Feast day: 20 August.

Symbols: a beehive; a pen and ink; a chained devil.

Patron: of beekeepers, honey and candle makers.

St Bernadette

Female variations: Berna, Bernardine, Bernarda, Bernarde, Berneta, Bernie, Berny, Bernice

There have been many other canonized Bernards and Barnardinos, but the best loved of their namesakes must be Bernardette Soubirous, the young shepherd girl who saw visions of Mary at Lourdes. Despite all the fuss which ensued, Bernadette never sought publicity for herself and lived out her short life in a convent at Nevers.

Feast day: 16 April.

Patron: of shepherds.

St Brigid

Meaning: **from Old Irish, 'strong'.**

Female variations: Brigid, Bedelia, Biddy, Birgitta, Bride, Brigitte, Britt, Gita

Brigid, born in Ireland about 450, became so beloved for her charity and her miracle-working powers that it is hard to piece together any factual account of her life. Nevertheless, she was born near Dundalk and founded a monastery at Kildare before her death in 525. *The Book of Lismore* says of her, 'everything that Brigid would ask of the Lord was granted at once, for this was her desire: to satisfy the poor, to drive out every hardship, to spare every miserable man ... She is the Mary of Gael.' Whether or not she hung her cloak on an obliging sunbeam, as the legend goes, is open to doubt, but that – and not the names and the dates – is what sticks so delightfully in the imagination.

Feast day: 1 February.

Symbols: a column of fire; a goose; a branch growing from an altar; a cow; a large bowl; corn; a book.

Patron: of dairymaids and poultry women, nuns, Ireland and New Zealand.

St Bridget

Bridget, born in Sweden nearly a 1000 years later than Brigid, could not have had a more different life. She was born into a wealthy family; her marriage produced eight children, one of whom (Katherine of Vadstena) was also to be canonized. She had a place at court and, after she was widowed, became a mystic and writer whose advice was accepted by kings and popes. She founded the Bridgettine Order for men and women at Vadstena, Sweden, but then left the country to travel on pilgrimage. Eventually, she settled in Rome where she worked among the poor. She died there in 1373.

Feast day: 23 July.

Patron: of scholars and Sweden.

St Bruno

Meaning: from Old German, 'brown'.

St Bruno the Great, son of St Matilda, was Archbishop of Cologne in 953, and a ruler of considerable power in the absence of his brother, the German Emperor Otto I.

It is St Bruno of Chartreuse (born in Cologne in 1030 and named after the Archbishop), however, who is much better known, for it was he who founded the great Carthusian monastery of La Grande Chartreuse. Bruno and six others lived much like the first Desert Fathers, in solitude and great poverty. Like his namesake, however, St Bruno was also called to public life – in this case as papal adviser to Urban II – and he was never allowed to return to his monastery. He died in 1101 in another monastery he founded called La Torre, in Calabria, Italy.

Feast day: 6 October.

Symbols: a flowering crucifix; a death's head; a star on his chest; seven stars.

Patron: of those who are victims of demonic possession.

C

St Catherine

Meaning: **from the Greek, 'pure, clean'.**

Female variations: Catharine, Caitlin, Cathy, Catriona, Cathryn, Cathleen, Caterina, Katherine, Kathryn, Karen, Kate, Kathleen, Katia, Katie, Katy, Kaye, Kit, Kitty, Trina

Of all the St Catherines, the most famous must be the highly romanticized Catherine of Alexandria, supposedly an Egyptian queen, whose beauty and philosophy attracted the attentions of the Emperor Maxentius. Having been converted to Christianity and – in a vision – mystically married to Christ, she did not reciprocate Maxentius' feelings. The Emperor, determined to win her for his wife, sent 50 philosophers to reason her out of her faith, but she out-argued them, and they were all executed. She was then tortured and imprisoned. One attempt to break her spirit was made by trying to break her body on a spiked wheel. Instead it was the wheel that broke, killing some of the spectators. In the end, Catherine was decapitated, although legend has it that it was milk and not blood which poured from her neck.

Feast day: 25 November.

Symbols: a broken wheel; a bridal veil; a ring.

Patron: of lawyers, librarians, students, philosophers and universities, as well as rope-makers, wheelwrights, and young girls.

There are many other St Catherines whose historicity is certain; of these, St Catherine of Siena is the most remarkable. Lay women were rarely canonized in past centuries; yet Catherine was not only canonized in 1461 but also declared a Doctor of the Church, even though she was illiterate. Although she was not a member of an Order, she became a Third Order Dominican and, in turn, attracted to herself a circle of admirers who were called the 'Caterinati', drawn from all walks of life. Gradually, Catherine became involved in the political and ecclesiastical scandal of the wars between Italian states and the Pope, and dictated many letters to religious and secular leaders, as well as mystical treatises. She received the stigmata, and once had a vision of her mystical marriage to Christ.

Feast day: 30 April.

Symbols: a lily; the stigmata and crown of thorns; a wedding ring.

Patron: of young girls, nurses and Italy.

St Cecilia

Meaning: **from the Latin, 'blind'.**

Variations: Cecil

Female variations: Cecille, Celine, Celia, Cis, Cicely, Cissie, Sheelagh, Sheila, Shelly, Zazilie, Zilla

Sadly, the legend of St Cecilia is now considered to be just another Christian romance. Perhaps, though, we should be thankful that this lady did not suffer the torments of being suffocated by the steam in her own bath, and then – when that proved useless – being left for three days to die of three sword strokes to her neck. The story is that Cecilia was a noble Roman Christian who vowed herself to virginity despite being married off to a man named Valerian. On their wedding night, she managed to convert him and he was subsequently martyred together with his brother and a friend before the authorities made their assault on Cecilia.

Of course, it is Cecilia's connection with music that we are most familiar with. According to the story, it was through (or despite) the wedding music that Cecilia prayed to God for help, and she has become the muse of church musicians ever since. Whether or not there ever was a Cecilia is impossible to say. It may be that she was the wealthy Roman Cecilia who founded a church in Rome and was given an honourable burial there. At all events, the inspiration and the music are real enough.

Feast day: 22 November.

Symbols: an organ; a lute; a harp; two wreaths of roses and lilies.

Patron: of musicians.

St Charles

Meaning: **from Old German, 'man'.**

Variations: Carl, Carlo, Carlos, Carroll, Caryl, Chick, Chuck, Karel, Karl

Female variations: Charlotte, Carlotta, Charlene, Lola, Lolita, Lotte, Lottie, Tottie, Carla, Carol, Cheryl

We still tend to think of saints and martyrs as medieval and white – or even Roman and white – whereas, in fact, this century and a half has seen more Christian martyrdoms than ever before, most of them in Third World countries. One of these, Charles Lwanga, was burned to death in 1886. He was one of many teenage boys kept by Mwanga, King of Uganda, in an 'alternative' harem. Charles became a Christian and converted 22 of his friends, whereupon they were transported to Namugongo and executed. He is remembered on 3 June and honoured as a patron of African boys.

The film *Black Robe* gave another side to the story of missionary stupidity and Amerindian sensitivity; Charles Garnier, a French priest who was murdered by the Iroquois while he was living and working in a

Huron village in 1649, might have been the inspiration for it. His feast day is the 26 September.

St Charles Borromeo, however, after whom so many of the other St Charles were named was indeed medieval and white. After the rather scandalous start of being born to a Medici and a Borromeo, and becoming the owner of a rich abbey and then a cardinal by nepotism (literally – the gift given by his uncle, Pope Pius IV) before he was 23, Charles became a priest and bishop in his own right. Although he had a stammer, he preached tirelessly, and set about reforming the Church so rigorously that a monk of the *Humilitati* (an Order which was losing money through these reforms), tried to assassinate him. When the plague broke out, he spent his energy and his personal fortune caring for the sick, and he also founded Sunday Schools or 'the Confraternity of Christian Doctrine'. If he had one indulgence, apparently it was the comparatively innocent one – at least by his ancestors' standards – for playing chess.

Feast day: 4 November.

Symbols: an orb and cross; the word *humilitas* (humility) with a crown.

Patron: of Sunday School teachers, ordinands and seminarians.

St Christina

Meaning: **from the Latin, 'Christian'.**

Variation: Christian

Female variations: Christiana, Christine, Chris, Christabel, Chrissie, Kirsten, Kirsty, Tina

St Christina the Astonishing is the most famous of several canonized Christinas, due to her peculiar psychic phenomena, all written down at the time by Cardinal James de Vitry. She was born in Liège, Belgium, in 1150; after a near-death experience – from which she 'awoke' at her own funeral Mass – she flew up into the rafters of the church, in disgust at the garlic-laden breath of the congregation. After her visions of hell and purgatory, she decided to give her life to prayer for the liberation of souls in purgatory, but the hypersensitivity to smell (especially the smell of men) never left her, and she went to extraordinary lengths (and heights) to avoid them.

Feast day: 24 July.

Patron: of psychiatrists.

St Christopher

Meaning: from the Greek, 'Christ-bearer'.

Variations: Chris, Chrissie, Christie, Chrystal,
Kester, Kit

Everyone has seen the little medals or car stickers
showing the patron saint of travellers, St Christopher.
Their use stems from the fact that Christopher, so the
story goes, was a giant of a man who longed to serve
the greatest master; he entered the service of a king,
but left it when he saw the king abase himself before
an evil wizard. Christopher then tried to serve the
Devil, but became disillusioned when he saw the Devil
cringe at the sight of a hermit's crucifix. The hermit
lived beside a river and scratched a living ferrying people across, so Christopher stayed to help him.

One dark and stormy night, a tiny child came to
Christopher and pleaded to be carried across. Against
his better judgement, the giant took the child and
entered the wild water. He found that he could barely
stand, while the weight of the child grew insupportable.
When he had struggled desperately to the other side,
the child told him that he was the Christ for whom
Christopher was looking, and that he had carried the
weight of the whole world on his shoulder.

Even if this story is not true, it illustrates the literal
meaning of the name 'Christophoros' (Christ-bearer)
which was borne by a martyr, probably in third-century
Asia Minor. St Christopher is still an important saint for
travellers; perhaps he should also give courage to the
growing numbers of unemployed people.

Feast day: 25 July.

Symbols: a Christ-child on his shoulder; a lantern; a palm tree and river.

Patron: of all people who travel or work with transport, as well as those in danger of water, storms or sudden death.

St Clare

Meaning: **from the Latin, 'bright'.**

Female variations: Claire, Clara, Chiara, Claribel, Clarice, Clarrie, Calinda, Clarissa

Clare, born in Assisi, Italy, scandalized her wealthy family – just as St Francis had – by taking her faith too seriously and running away from them to live with Francis, his fellow monks and 'Lady Poverty' for the love of God. Of course, the free Franciscan life on the road was not suitable for a lady of that time, and Clare had to be content to lead her own Order of 'Poor Ladies' in the church of San Damiano, with a Rule written for her by St Francis.

Although she and her sisters could not travel with Francis, they shared his devotion to Christ, and insisted on living in the greatest poverty. They embroidered church vestments and linen, and gave their enclosed lives to prayer. Clare herself seems to have been as loved by her sisters as Francis was by his followers. Franciscan austerity was never imposed on other people, but it seems to have given freedom and joy to anyone who dared to risk it.

Feast day: 12 August.

Symbols: a chalice and host; a tall cross; a monstrance (the special gold or silver container for displaying the wafer for Holy Communion); a lily; a ciborium (the covered chalice in which the wafer for Holy Communion is kept).

Patron: of embroiderers and those with eye troubles; also of television – either because her name means 'light' or because one Christmas she was given a vision of the stable in Bethlehem.

St Clement

Meaning: from the Latin, 'merciful'.

Female variations: Clementine, Clementia, Clementina, Clemency, Clem

The Clement from whom all other St Clements take their name was the fourth Pope, coming after Peter, Linus and Cletus. St Irenaeus tells us that '[Clement] had seen and consorted with the blessed apostles'; he may be the Clement mentioned in Philippians 4:3, but we do not know very much about his life. What we do have is his letter to the Corinthians, dealing with the troubled affairs of their Church. Legends abound about him being sent to the marble mines of Russia and eventually martyred by being tied to an anchor and thrown into the sea. It is said that his tomb on the sea bed, made by angels, can be seen once a year at exceptionally low tides.

Feast day: 23 November.

Symbols: a fountain; an anchor; a tiara; a maniple (an ornamental band worn on the left arm by the celebrant at Communion); a marble temple in the sea.

Patron: of lighthouses, stonecutters and blacksmiths.

St Crispin

Meaning: **from the Latin, 'curled'.**

Variations: Crispinian, Crispianius, Crispian

Crispin was a Roman shoemaker, together with his brother, Crispinian. They set out on a missionary expedition to France with St Quentin but were martyred at Soissons in 285. According to legend, their bodies were thrown into the sea and eventually found their way to Faversham in Kent. It may be that they were martyred in Rome, in fact, and their relics were brought to Soissons. Whatever the truth, they are still venerated as the patron saints of shoemakers and leather workers.

Feast day: 25 October.

Symbols: a shoe; a last (the wooden or metal form on which a shoe is fashioned).

Patron: of leather workers and cobblers.

St Crispina

Crispina was also martyred in the Roman persecutions. She was a Numidian woman, married and with children, who refused to sacrifice to pagan gods on behalf of the Emperor and was therefore beheaded. Accounts of her trial exist, and she is mentioned several times by St Augustine. Her feast day is 5 December.

D

St Damian

Meaning: from the Greek, a 'tamer' or 'guide'.

Variations: Damyan, Dami, Damien, Damon

Like Crispin, Damian had a fraternal companion – Cosmas – although the names of Crispinian and Cosmas have not been as popular as their brothers'. Cosmas and Damian were highly venerated martyrs in the Eastern Church as twin brothers from Syria who practised medicine and refused to accept fees for their help.

Feast day: 27 September.

Symbols: arrows; phials and jars; the rod of Aesculapius (the Roman god of medicine or healing).

Patron: of doctors, dentists, barbers and pharmacists.

St Daniel

Meaning: from the Hebrew, 'God has judged'.

Variations: Danny, Dan, Deiniol

Female variations: Danielle, Daniella

Most Christians, perhaps, named in honour of Daniel are named after the Old Testament prophet who outfaced the lions in their den and who had such strange visions. There are actually three St Daniels named after him: one, a medieval missionary to the Moors during the crusades; another, a French missionary to Senegal whose special love was for orphans, who died in 1936.

The third, the most famous Daniel of all, was the Stylite (or pillar-saint) who lived in the fifth century. He lived a perfectly ordinary monk's life until he paid two visits to Simon the Stylite, who lived as a hermit on top of a 60-foot pillar on Mount Telanissae. It fired his enthusiasm so much that he was ordained on top of a pillar of his own, given to him by the Emperor Leo I, and lived there for 33 years. He came down only once, to reprimand the Emperor Basilicus for supporting a heretical doctrine. Otherwise, he lived atop his pillar, healing the sick, giving spiritual direction and preaching very good sermons.

Feast day: 11 December.

Symbols: a tall pillar.

St David

Meaning: **from the Hebrew, 'darling' or 'friend'.**

Variations: Dai, Dafydd, Dave, Davin, Davy, Dewi

Female variations: Davina, Davida, Davidina, Davinia, Davita, Veda, Vida, Vita

David is an Old Testament name, but its popularity is largely due to a Welsh saint, Dewi, known to non-Welsh speakers as 'David'. There are other canonized Davids, notably a Scottish king of the twelfth century, but it is St David of Wales who is the best known. This David is reputed, in some historical accounts, to have descended from King Arthur; he was certainly revered all over the Celtic region. He became the first bishop in South Wales, and founded a series of monasteries of extreme austerity – so much so that some accused him of being more in love with asceticism than Christ. His nickname ('the waterman'), may derive from the fact that his rule forbade the drinking of wine; the tradition that he ate only bread and leeks (hence the Welsh emblem) is apocryphal.

Feast day: 1 March.

Symbols: a dove on a shoulder; a leek; a harp; a hill; fountains.

Patron: of poetry and Wales.

St Dominic

Meaning: **from the Latin, 'of the Lord'.**

Variations: Dom, Domenic, Domingo, Nick, Nicky

Female variations: Dominica, Dominique

Although there were several early martyrs called Dominica, it was the twelfth-century St Dominic who inspired many more Dominics to become saints and martyrs. Dominic was a Spaniard whose religious energy sprang from his fights against heresy. Before he was born, his mother had a vision in which she saw her son as a dog holding a flaming torch; the nickname of the Dominican Order came to be 'the hounds of God'. Later, when he was christened, she saw a star shining on him. Dominic was to be, with Francis, the most influential saint of his era.

Dominic's first foundation was a convent for French nuns who had renounced the Albigensian heresy. For the rest of his life, he established and directed the Order of Preachers, the great counterpart to Francis' order. Between the two men, Western Christianity was reformed and rejuvenated by dusty friars travelling in poverty and preaching to ordinary people all over Europe. The popular image of Dominic was of a man as ruthless as the terrible Inquisitions of the Cathars and Albigensians, which he supported, but apparently he was a hugely compassionate and intellectual man. He remained true to his ideal of personal poverty, dying in a borrowed habit and a borrowed bed because he possessed none of his own.

Feast day: 8 August.

Symbols: a lily; a greyhound; a book; a star on his forehead; a rosary; a dog holding a torch.

Patron: of astronomy, friars, preachers and the Dominican Republic.

St Dorothy

Meaning: **from the Greek, 'gift of God'.**

Female variations: Dorothea, Dodie, Dolly, Dora, Doreen, Dorinda, Dorrit, Dory, Dot, Dottie

The martyr of the Diocletian persecution is a Christian heroine of a romance. The story goes that she was a beautiful girl of Cappadocia (Turkey) who was sentenced to death. As she was being led out to execution, a lawyer, Theophilus, jeered at her, asking her to send him fruit and flowers from the heavenly garden. After her death, a child appeared to him with a basket of roses and apples, adding – ominously – that Dorothy was waiting for him in the garden. Theophilus was converted, and immediately executed too.

Feast day: 6 February.

Symbols: an angel with a basket of apples or roses; a sword; a crown.

Patron: of florists and gardeners.

E

St Edmund

Meaning: **from Old English, 'rich guardian'.**

Variations: Eamon, Ed, Eddie, Edmond, Ned, Ted, Teddy

St Edmund is largely forgotten now, except in the town of Bury St Edmunds, Suffolk, where he is buried. But Edmund, King of the Angles and martyr, was once one of the greatest English saints and his shrine one of the richest in medieval Europe. The story of his martyrdom varies, but the best telling of it is by Julian Tennyson (*Suffolk Scene*, Alistair Press, 1987), one of Edmund's countrymen in our own century. The bare bones of it is that Edmund, the boy King, tried to defend his country from marauding Danes and was captured. Refusing to compromise his faith or the well-being of his people, Edmund was shot through with arrows in 870. The Danes then cut off his head and threw it away, but a wolf guarded it until it was discovered and reunited with his body.

Feast day: 20 November.

Symbols: arrows; a cudgel; a wolf.

Patron: of East Anglia and wolves.

St Edward

Meaning: **from Old English, 'rich guardian'.**

Variations: Ed, Eddie, Ned, Neddy, Ted, Teddy

The first King Edward to be canonized was the unfortunate lad who, about a 100 years after Edmund met his death, was murdered at the age of 16. Whether or not this was really a martyrdom, people reported many miracles happening about his grave and he was canonized soon after. His feast day is on the 18 March.

Edward the Confessor is chiefly remembered as the gentle but wise and effective king who succeeded to the throne of England in 1042. Even before his death, he was venerated for his holiness; it was of him that it was first said that to touch the King would cure scrofula, 'the King's evil'. Westminster Abbey is the beautiful church that we know today because of Edward's love for it. He refounded the small monastery, as it was then, and greatly enlarged the church where he, at his own wish, was buried on his death in 1066.

Feast day: 13 October.

Symbols: a ring in his hand; a sceptre with a dove; a purse.

St Elizabeth

Meaning: from the Hebrew, 'God is my satisfaction'.

Female variations: Babette, Belle, Bess, Bessie, Beth, Betsy, Bettee, Bettina, Betty, Elisabeth, Eliza, Elly, Elsa, Elsie, Elspeth, Elise, Isabel, Isabella, Isobel, Ysabel, Libby, Libbie, Lib, Lillibet, Lisa, Lise, Liselotte, Lisette, Liz, Lizzie, Lizzy

The first Elizabeth in the Christian calendar was the cousin of Mary, and the mother of St John the Baptist. The story of her miraculous conception of John is told in the first pages of the Gospel according to St Luke, and it mirrors the yet more miraculous birth of Christ. There are other traditions about her and her husband, Zachariah; whatever the truth of them, she is invoked as the patroness of all pregnant women for it was while he was in her womb that John first 'leaped' in joyful recognition of Jesus.

Feast day: 5 November.

Symbols: Elizabeth herself greeting Mary and/or holding John the Baptist.

Patron: of pregnant women.

There have been many other St Elizabeths since. One was Queen Elizabeth of Hungary, whose unhappy life as wife, mother and queen was matched only by that of her great-niece, Queen Elizabeth of Portugal. Elizabeth of Hungary is remembered for her unceasing charity to the poor in spite of her husband's opposition and then, after his death, her own poverty. She died at the age of 24 in 1231. Her symbols are three crowns (as virgin, wife and widow) and roses, a basket of bread, a baby in a cradle, a distaff, and bread and wine. Her feast day is on 19 November. A later Elizabeth was the first American-born to be canonized. Elizabeth Bayley Seton was born in 1774, was married and the mother of five children. Before her husband's death she founded a Protestant charity for women and children; after he died she became a Roman Catholic and founded a girls' school. She then became 'Mother Seton', the Mother Superior of a new Order of nuns called the Daughters of Charity of St Joseph. Her feast day is on 4 January.

St Emily

Meaning: **from the Roman clan, Aemelius.**

Variations: Emil

Female variations: Em, Emalia, Emilia, Emmie, Emmy, Emilie

One account of the first Blessed Emily tells that she was the first prioress of the first house of Dominican regular Tertiaries. She was, at any rate, an Italian woman of the thirteenth century whose reputation of goodness – some say miracle-working power – has come down to us today. She is remembered on 19 August. Another Emily that followed her is Emily de

Rodat, a Frenchwoman who had a sad and difficult life which, to some, made her a sad and difficult person. Nevertheless, in 1815 she opened a free school in Villefranche-de-Rouergue which became the congregation of the Holy Family at Villefranche and spread to other countries. Her feast day is on 19 September.

Another St Emily is also a Frenchwoman, Emily de Vialar, who founded the Sisters of St Joseph 'of the Apparition' in 1832. Despite her good work in her second foundation in Algeria, she was harried by its Archbishop, excommunicated and driven out of the country. Emily was proved innocent, however, and the Order flourished, becoming internationally known for its charity and care of children. She herself was regarded as wise, sensitive and utterly dedicated to her work, despite her own physical disabilities. Her feast day is on 17 June.

St Emma

Meaning: from Old German, 'universal'.

Female variations: Em, Emmie, Erma, Imma, Irma

Little is known of St Emma, who died in 1045, apart from the sad circumstances of her life. She was happily married to the Landgrave of Friesach, Austria, and had two sons, but they were murdered and her husband died while away on a journey. Unlike many of the women who later became saints, widowhood was not delicious freedom but a terrible blow to Emma. She later founded a double monastery in Carinthia, Austria, and her feast day is celebrated on 30 June.

St Eric

Meaning: from Old Norse, 'ever ruling'.

Variations: Erick, Rick, Rickie, Ricky

Female variations: Erica, Erika, Rickie, Rikkie

Eric IX became King of Sweden in 1150. He was a very pious, good, Christian man and systematically set about ensuring that not only his own subjects but also the neighbouring heathen Finns became Christians too. He codified Swedish law, and built the first Swedish cathedral in Uppsala. He also defended his country against Finnish attack. Unfortunately, he was murdered in 1161 by a band of Danes, abetted by some of his own treacherous countrymen.

Feast day: 18 May.

Symbols: three crowns and a banner; a fountain.

Patron: of Sweden.

F

St Felix

Meaning: **from the Latin, 'fortunate' and 'happiness'.**

There are over 60 saints called Felix recognized as martyrs by the Roman Catholic Church, but one of special interest to English people is the Burgundian who came as a missionary preacher to East Anglia and later became Bishop of Dunwich, the mysterious cathedral town which was washed into the sea. He also gave his name to the port of Felixstowe. He died in 648, and his feast day is kept on 8 March.

Felix of Nola lived three centuries earlier, near Naples, and became chaplain to his Bishop, Maximus. During the persecutions carried out by Emperor Decius (249–251), Maximus went into hiding, but Felix was arrested and tortured until he escaped with the help of an angel. He, too, was forced to hide from his pursuers; he succeeded this time with the help of a spider which spun a web covering the entrance of the cave in which he hid. Later, he found Bishop Maximus and looked after him until he died, but he refused to be consecrated bishop himself. He was known for his generosity and compassion and, after his death, great miracle-working power.

Feast day: 14 January.

Symbols: a cluster of grapes; an angel; a spider's web.

Patron: of all those who have been falsely accused.

St Felicity

Female variations: Felicia, Felice

The best-known Felicity (one of the few women saints named in the Roman Mass), was the slave girl of a wealthy Carthaginian woman named Perpetua. She and her mistress were arrested in 202 and faced certain death for their faith. The only question was whether Felicity might not be spared since she was pregnant. Eager to face martyrdom with her mistress, Felicity prayed and was brought into premature labour, giving birth to a son. Touched by their faith, the prison governor was converted, but they were nevertheless both tortured and killed by wild beasts.

Feast day: 6 March.

Patron: of mothers and infertile women.

St Flora

Meaning: **Roman goddess of flowers or Spring.**

Female variations: Fleur, Floella, Florella, Floretta, Florai, Floriane, Floris, Florrie

St Flora and St Mary are honoured on 24 November for their refusal to give up their faith during the persecution of Christians by the Moors in Spain. They were beheaded in Cordoba in 851. A later Flora (of Beaulieu) was a sister of the Order of St John of Jerusalem, near Rocamadour in France, but the strange accounts of her spiritual life are uncertain. She died in 1347 and her feast day is 5 October.

St Frances

Meaning: **from the Latin, 'from France' or 'a free citizen'.**

Female variations: Frances, Francesca, Fan, Fanny, Francine, Françoise, Frank, Franny, Zissie

Frances Xavier Cabrini was the first citizen of the USA to be canonized, although she was Italian, born in 1850. Her first Order was one of missionary nuns in Lombardy; she was then sent to America by Pope Leo XIII. Once there, Frances founded an orphanage for the children of Italian immigrants at West Park, and hospitals in New York and Chicago. She continued working throughout the American continent in Nicaragua, Chile, Argentina, Brazil and Costa Rica, until her death in 1917 in Chicago.

Feast day: 13 November.

Patron: of hospital managers, emigrants and immigrants.

St Francis

Variations: Fran, Frank, Franklin

Francis of Assisi was the first saint from which very many have taken their names, although 'Francesco' was just a nickname. Born in 1181, Francis (or John) was dazzled not only by the courtly romances of France, but by chivalry and adventure too. However, his *joie de vivre* and imagination were caught up in a completely new adventure: that of trying to live the Gospel as it was actually written. It sounds simple but in medieval Italy it was revolutionary.

Although Francis' family were Christians, they were not prepared to see their wealth given away impulsively. Francis kissed lepers, delighted in being mocked or even attacked, lived only on what he was given as alms, and took God's command to rebuild his Church equally literally: he found a small ruined church and began to restore it, stone by stone. The friars who joined him, the animals and birds who heard him preach, the women who formed his second Order of 'Poor Clares' and the many ordinary people who became Tertiaries all show how Francis' extraordinary gifts and determination to live the Gospel as perfectly as possible did, indeed, rebuild the Church in the twelfth century. He was the first saint to experience the strange phenomenon of the stigmata – Christ's wounds on the Cross – on his own body. The influence of Francis is still being felt in the Church today, especially where it works to protect the natural world or help the poor.

Feast day: 4 October.

Symbols: birds; animals; a winged crucifix with five rays; a crown of thorns; a lighted lamp; fine clothes and a bag of gold at his feet.

Patron: of birds and animals, the Green movement and Italy.

G

St Gabriel

Meaning: from the Hebrew, 'strong man of God'.

Variations: Gabby, Gabe

Female variations: Gabrielle, Gabriella, Gabby, Gabey

When people want to suggest someone who is absolutely perfect, they often invoke the archangel Gabriel who does, of course, have the edge on most saints simply by virtue of being an archangel. It was Gabriel who announced God's plan of action for the salvation of the world to the Virgin Mary, but he had previously appeared to Daniel and to Zachariah, and at the birth of Christ he led the angels in their exultant *Gloria in excelsis Deo!* Because of this, Gabriel is thought of as the communicator *in excelsis* and is the patron of all who work in communications. He is also honoured by Muslims as the one who dictated the Koran to Mohammed.

Feast day: 24 March.

Patron: of diplomats, communications workers; women in childbirth.

St Gemma

Meaning: **from the Latin, 'jewel'.**

Gemma Galgani was a young Tuscan servant, born in 1878 to a poor pharmacist. She longed to enter the order of the Passionist nuns, but was chronically ill with spinal tuberculosis. Although she later believed that she had been cured miraculously by the intervention of St Gabriel Possenti, she was still too weak. Nevertheless, she led an extraordinary life – alternating between mystical and demonic states, receiving the marks of the stigmata and often behaving in a way she could only explain as being possessed by demons. In between these periods, Gemma was considered to be exceptionally holy and patient in her suffering, and it was for these qualities that she was canonized after her death at the age of 25.

Feast day: 11 April.

Patron: of pharmacists.

St George

Meaning: **from the Greek, 'farmer'.**

Variations: Dod, Doddy, Geordie, Yorick

Female variations: Georgia, Georgette, Georgiana, Georgina, Georgie, Gina

There is so much scepticism about the story of George and the dragon that many people have begun to doubt his very existence, but it is probable that St George was a soldier of the third or fourth century, martyred in the Diocletian persecutions at Lydda in Palestine. Certainly, he became a widely venerated saint, especially among soldiers, and especially in the Eastern Church. The legend about the princess and the dragon was probably added in the medieval period, fond as people then were about stories of chivalry and romance. According to legend, George was a knight from Cappadocia who, when travelling through Silene in Libya, heard that the princess was to be the next victim of a fierce dragon which was gradually devouring all the young virgins of the place. George offered to go to the dragon in her place. There was a bloody fight between George and the dragon, but the former beheaded the latter, and the townspeople were so impressed that thousands became Christians on that day.

True or not, it is a story about courage and goodness which still catches the imagination, and the English still stoutly claim his patronage, even though the Roman Catholic Church has demoted him from its canon.

Feast day: 23 April.

Symbols: a dead dragon; a broken wheel; a white flag with a red cross.

Patron: of knights and soldiers (especially cavalry), Boy Scouts, riders, England, Portugal and Germany.

St Gerald

Meaning: from Old German, 'spear rule'.

Variations: Gary, Gerrie, Gerry, Jerold, Jerrie, Jerry,

Female variations: Geralda, Geraldine, Gerrie, Gerry, Jerrie, Jerry

Gerald of Aurillac, France, is one of the few laymen canonized for the holiness of his daily life. He was born in 855 into the aristocracy, and would later administer his estates with justice, great generosity and compassion for the poor. Although he did not feel free enough to renounce the world himself, he lived according to a rule, and founded a Benedictine monastery. His feast day is 13 October. Another Frenchman, Gerald of Sauve-Majeure, lived in the eleventh century. He first became Abbot at Laon, and then – finding the Rule there too lax – at his own foundation at Sauve-Majeure. His feast day is 5 April.

St Gilbert

Meaning: from Old German, 'bright pledge'.

Variations: Bert, Bertie, Berty, Gib, Gibb, Gil

Female variations: Gilberta, Gilberte

Gilbert of Sempringham is particularly interesting because he founded the only medieval Order which originated in England – the 'Gilbertines' – and also because he lived to the age of 106 at a time when the average life expectancy was about a quarter of that. Gilbert was born in Sempringham, Lincolnshire, in 1189 and became the vicar of the parish. A while later, when seven women asked him to write a Rule for them to live in community there, Gilbert initiated a widespread Order of men and women, lay and ordained, for work in hospitals and orphanages. Gilbert seems to have been a man of courage – he dared to help St Thomas à Becket in his quarrel with King Henry II – and a man of humility as well, for when he went blind in his old age, he was content to step down as Abbot and live on in his community as an ordinary brother.

Feast day: 16 February.

Symbol: a model of a church.

St Giles

Meaning: **from the Greek, 'a kid'.**

Variations: Aegidius, Egidius, Gyles

Female variations: Egidia, Giles

St Giles, a much-loved saint in Britain, is one of the medieval saints who are particularly associated with animals. The story goes that he was a French hermit living in Saint-Gilles, near Arles, before the ninth century. He used to be fed by a deer, who gave him her milk. One day, however, King Wamba of the Visigoths came crashing through the forest on a hunt; the deer sought refuge with Giles and sheltered in the saint's arms; the king tried to shoot the deer but found he had shot and wounded St Giles instead. Perhaps out of remorse, Wamba gave Giles land on which he subsequently built a monastery.

Feast day: 1 September.

Symbol: a red deer killed with arrows.

Patron: of cripples and beggars, breastfeeding mothers, and hermits. He is also invoked by women who wish to conceive.

St Gregory

Meaning: from the Greek, 'watchman'.

Variations: Gregor, Greer, Greg, Gregg

Female variations: Greer, Gregoria

Gregory (540–604) is one of the great figures in the Western Church. Born into a wealthy family and becoming a very successful chief civil magistrate in Rome, he subsequently devoted much of his wealth to the founding of monasteries, eventually renouncing his worldly life and becoming a monk. Ten years later, in 590, he was the first monk ever to be elected Pope.

Perhaps his most famous saying was made on passing through the slave market. He was admiring some blond children and asked of what race they came. On being told that they were Angles, he protested, 'Not Angles but angels!' On learning that the Angles of England were pagans, he put plans in order that Augustine should lead a mission there.

He has affected our lives in many ways, being a keen statesman and having had a great influence on the emerging Europe in his time. He shaped the way clergy – especially bishops – came to see their ministry and famously reorganized the Church's patterns of worship and music. What we know as the 'Gregorian chant' was written down and systematized under his supervision.

Feast day: 3 September.

Symbols: a dove; an altar; an ancient manuscript of music.

Patron: of music, Popes and schools.

St Guy

Meaning: **from the Latin, 'life'; from Old German, 'wood' or 'wild'.**

Guy of Anderlecht was a Belgian peasant in the tenth century who, poor though he was, resolved to renounce the pursuit of money and become a hermit. He eventually became the sacristan of a church at Laecken, where he lived happily until he was persuaded by a merchant to invest the little money he had left. His hope was that it would raise money to help the poor, but it ended disastrously with the ship his goods were on, going down. Thoroughly disillusioned. Guy left Laeken on a pilgrimage and spent years wandering through Europe to Rome and Jerusalem, returning to Laeken to die. Although he is credited with many miracles, it was the events surrounding his burial at Anderlecht which seemed to confirm his local popularity. When a horse kicked his grave (or did something even less respectful, according to some sources) it was immediately struck dead. This makes him, oddly enough, the patron saint of horses.

Feast day: 12 September.

Patron: of horses.

H

St Helen

Meaning: **from the Greek, 'bright'.**

Female variations: **Aileen, Eileen, Elaine, Eleanor, Elena, Elinor, Ella, Ellen, Ellie, Helena, Ilene, Lana, Lena, Leonora, Nell, Nellie, Nelly**

St Helen is always thought of as the woman who found the Cross on which Christ was crucified. Born in about 255 in Drepanum, Asia Minor, Helen was probably just an ordinary, poor girl until she happened to attract the attention of a Roman officer stationed there called Constantius. She went with him to Rome and gave birth to a son. More was to come, however, for Constantius became Emperor, and tried to divorce his humble wife, banishing her from Rome. When Helen's son Constantine inherited his father's empire, Helen was brought back again and crowned as an empress.

Constantine won a famous victory after having had a vision of the Cross of Christ; after that, Christianity became legal in the Roman Empire. Helen embraced the faith and went on pilgrimage to the Holy Land where she studied the ancient sites and founded many churches, as well as helping the poor. Whether or not the story is true about her finding the Cross buried near Calvary, and finding the nails and seamless robe, her faith, devotion and charity are undoubted.

Feast day: 18 August.

Symbols: a crown; a cross; a hammer and nails; an open book and a crown.

Patron: of archaeologists.

St Henry

Meaning: from Old German, 'home ruler'.

Variations: Hal, Hank, Harry

Female variations: Etta, Ettie, Hattie, Henrietta, Hettie, Hetty

Henry II (born in 973), was a Bavarian prince and later Holy Roman Emperor. His tutor was St Wolfgang of Regensburg; Henry apparently had a vision of Wolfgang after his death, portending his own coronation. He was also a friend of St Odilo of Cluny and it was said that he, too, wanted to be a monk, and therefore never consummated his marriage with St Cunegund. It seems that Henry worked with zeal for German unity and the Church's reorganization.

Feast day: 13 July.

Symbols: a sword and a church; a lily; a crown; a dove on an orb.

Patron: of Finland.

St Hilary

Meaning: **from the Latin, 'cheerful'.**

Variation: Hilaire

Female variations: Hilaira, Illaria, Yllaria

There were five Hilarys canonized in the early Church, but it is Hilary of Poitiers who is best known to us, giving his name to the second term in the academic year – the Hilary Term – to the Law Courts and some universities; this, as the Spring term, would begin around the time of his feast day. Hilary was born about 315 into a wealthy pagan family of Poitiers; after his conversion to Christianity he was consecrated as Bishop (although he was married and a father). He is chiefly remembered for his great theological writings against the Arian heresy which was exercising the Church at that time. Arius taught that Jesus Christ was human, not divine, whereas orthodox Christianity has always believed Jesus Christ to be both human and divine. In fact, Hilary was such a fierce defender of the Trinity that he was exiled from his diocese and sent to Phrygia by the Emperor Constantius II (who happened to be an Arian himself). This ploy backfired, for Hilary proceeded to dig deeper into Greek theology, becoming even more convinced by orthodox Christian doctrine – and was not afraid to say so. In the end, the Arians sent him back to his diocese, labelling him a 'mischief-maker'.

After he died, his bed was set up in the cathedral of Poitiers and was known as 'Hilary's Cradle'. It was thought that anyone who could be made to sleep a night in it would be cured of insanity. Hilary also was reputed to have cleared an island of snakes, and thus is often invoked against snakebite.

Feast day: 13 or 14 January.

Symbols: a child in a cradle; a trumpet; the serpent on a stick.

Patron: of slow learners, the mentally ill, and lawyers.

St Hilda

Meaning: from Old German, 'battle'.

Female variations: Hide, Hildy, Hylda

Hilda was a noblewoman of Northumbria, christened at the age of 13 with her great-uncle, King Edwin, in 627. Her vocation to the religious life came relatively late, but when she was 33 she was installed as Abbess of a convent in Hartlepool by St Aidan. Shortly after this, Hilda founded a double monastery at Whitby which became one of the largest and most important religious foundations in Britain. The Venerable Bede writes about her and some of the eminent people who lived there, including St John of Beverley and Caedmon, believed to be the author of the first English religious lyrics. An historic conference took place at Whitby in 664 to decide whether the English Church should follow the Celtic or Roman Church calendar. Apart from being formidably efficient and wise, Hilda was also very lovable, according to Bede.

Feast day: 17 November.

Symbols: snakes; a bird; a crosier; a model of Whitby Abbey.

St Hugh

Meaning: **from Old German, 'understanding'.**

Variations: Hew, Huey, Hughie, Hugo, Hughes, Huw

Female variation: Huguette

St Hugh of Grenoble was the beloved bishop of that city, whose personal holiness was combined with a great determination to improve both the practical and devotional life of the people in his care. He was once a pupil of St Bruno, and it was he who gave Bruno and his companions the land to build the great Cistercian monastery at La Grande Chartreuse. His feast day is celebrated on April Fools' Day and his symbols in art are a branch and seven stars, lanterns or three flowers.

St Hugh of Lincoln was, despite his name, another Frenchman, born in 1135 – three years after his compatriot's death. Like many other bishops, Hugh was appointed by a king hopeful of making friends in high places; like many other kings, Henry II was disappointed. In fact, Hugh turned out to be so firm in the defence of his people against the greed and arrogance of their royal masters that he was called 'Hammerking'. He may have called himself 'peppery' but he was greatly admired for his courage in standing up to Henry II, Richard and John. Not only did he fight royal oppression but he was remarkable for his defence of the Jews in his city at a time when persecution was common. He was known as a kind and tender man with time for the poor, for playing with children and caring for the ill. He kept many pets, including a wild swan who would bury its head in Hugh's wide sleeves and follow him everywhere about his manor, returning to the wild when Hugh was away from home.

Feast day: 17 November.

Symbol: a swan.

Patron: of swans.

St James

Meaning: **from the Hebrew, 'Jacob' or 'heel-grabber'.**

Variations: **Hamish, Jake, Jamey, Jamie, Jay, Jem, Jemmy, Jim, Jimmy, Seamus**

Female variations: **Jamesina, Jacoba, Jacqueline, Jacquetta, Jackie, Jacklyn**

While Jacob is one of the Old Testament heroes whose very name – 'heel-grabber' – tells us that he was not very saintly, there are two James in the New Testament – the Greater and the Lesser – who became saints and apostles. James the Greater is perhaps more familiar, being the brother of John, son of Zebedee, and one of the inner circle of disciples. Some believe that James and John may even have been cousins of Jesus, if Salome, their mother, was Mary's sister. James and John, together with Peter, were the disciples who Jesus called to witness his Transfiguration and to be with him during his agony in the Garden of Gethsemane. The Acts of the Apostles tells us that James was the first of the Twelve to be martyred – he was executed by King

Herod Agrippa I in 44. The legend is that his body was miraculously transferred to Santiago de Compostela, Spain. The great cathedral there became, with Jerusalem and Rome, one of the main centres of pilgrimage, so that James' symbol, the cockleshell, became the badge of all pilgrims.

Feast day: 25 July.

Symbols: a pilgrim's staff, hat, cloak, wallet, purse and cockleshell; keys; a white horse and white flag.

Patron: of soldiers and cavalry, vets, furriers, Spain, Guatemala and Nicaragua.

St James the Lesser is so called because he was younger than James, son of Zebedee; no slur on his saintliness is intended. Although he was not one of the three who were closest to Jesus, many people think he was the James – 'the Lord's brother' – mentioned several times in the New Testament. Whatever the case, it was he who became the leader of the Church in Jerusalem after the Resurrection. He was stoned to death in about 62.

Feast day: 1 May.

Symbols: a windmill; a halbert (weapon); three stones; bread.

Patron: of the dying.

St Jane

Meaning: **from the Hebrew, 'Jehovah has favoured' or 'John'.**

Female variations: Jan, Janet, Janey, Janie, Janice, Joan, Sheena, Sheenagh, Sian, Sine, Sinead

Jane is one of the feminine forms of John, so a Jane or Joan might take one of the many St Johns for her patron. There is, however, a very attractive St Jane whose life might be an inspiration for any woman because it combined marriage and motherhood with great holiness and administrative skill. Jane Frances de Chantal (1572–1641) was a well-born frenchwoman of Dijon. She married when she was 20, and had four children; unfortunately, after eight happy years, she was widowed. She later began to develop her spiritual life under the direction of St François de Sales. Three years later, he asked her to become the Superior of a new Order for women which would foster the vocations of widows like herself, or women whose age or health would not permit them to join other, more austere orders. Therefore, Jane became the foundress of the Order of the Visitation; it grew so fast that there were 80 houses by the time she died. Jane was the grand-mother of that bubbly woman of letters, Madame de Sevigny; according to St Vincent de Paul, Jane was 'one of the holiest people I have ever met on this earth'.

Feast day: 21 August.

St Jerome

Meaning: **from the Greek, 'sacred name'.**

Variations: Gerrie, Gerry, Jerry

St Jerome is the saint always portrayed with a lion because of the delightful story about how he bravely removed a thorn from its paw, setting the lion to watch over his recalcitrant donkey. Jerome was not just a desert hermit and animal lover, however. He is also remembered as a Doctor of the Church because of his outstanding scholarship. In 382, Jerome became secretary to Pope St Damasus, who set him the extraordinary labour of translating the Greek and Hebrew books of the Bible into Latin, which was becoming the universal language of the Church. Although he was notoriously vitriolic about marriage, Jerome conceived a great friendship for a Roman widow, Paula, and her daughters, and they went to live in Bethlehem. With Paula's money, they were able to found a double monastery, hospice and school. He died there in 420.

Feast day: 30 September.

Symbols: a lion; an inkhorn and pen; a fox; a hare; a partridge; an open Bible; a fawn.

Patron: of librarians and scholars.

St Joan

Meaning: **from the Hebrew, 'Jehovah has favoured'.**

Female variations: Jan, Janet, Janice, Janie, Janine, Jean, Jeanette, Jennet, Jennie, Jenny, Jessie, Jinny, Joanna, Joanne, Joni, Netta, Nettie, Sheena, Sian, Sine, Sinead, Siobhan

Joan is the name of several French saints, the most famous of whom is, of course, Joan of Arc. This illiterate teenage peasant girl was prompted by heavenly voices, those of St Michael, St Catherine and St Margaret, to crown the Dauphin at Rheims and to lead his troops into battle. When Charles VII's courage failed, things went against the French. Joan was captured by the Burgundians, who were allied with the English, and sold to them for a 'show trial'. It is often forgotten, however, that her canonization was not for her patriotism or her courage, but her faithfulness and obedience to God. She was only 19 when she chose death by burning rather than having to collude with political lies.

Feast day: 30 May.

Symbol: a fleur-de-lys, armour; a sword; a flag with the fleur-de-lys; a tunic; a stake.

Patron: of France.

St John

Meaning: from the Hebrew, 'Jehovah has favoured'.

Variations: Evan, Ewan, Iain, Ian, Jack, Jan, Jevan, Jock, Johnny, Owen, Sean, Shaun, Zane

There are at least 64 Johns in Roman martyrology, as well as many other fascinating characters like the Curé d'Ars, and St John of the Cross; the number of different forms of the name show how popular it was and still is. But it was from St John the Apostle and Evangelist and, to a lesser extent, St John the Baptist, that all Johns take their inspiration.

St John the Evangelist was the brother of James, son of Zebedee and Salome, and perhaps even the cousin of Jesus. He was certainly one of the three disciples who were called to be with Jesus during his Transfiguration and the agony in the Garden of Gethsemane, and tradition has it that he was 'the disciple whom Jesus loved', mentioned in his Gospel. It was he who received Jesus' charge to look after Mary, his mother, and he who, as tradition has it, gave us the majestic fourth Gospel, as well as other letters in the New Testament. It is said that he lived for many years on Patmos, Greece, and later at Ephesus, Turkey, where he died.

Feast day: 27 December.

Symbols: a cup and a serpent; an eagle; a serpent on a sword; a scroll of his Gospel.

Patron: of writers and Turkey.

John the Baptist has a rather different reputation from that of the gentle old man of Ephesus. Luke's Gospel account certainly portrays him as the cousin of Jesus, but he seems to have been a rough and ready man. As a baby in the womb, he greeted Jesus, and became the voice crying in the wilderness: 'prepare ye the way of the Lord', as foretold in Malachi 3:1. His life baptizing people in the Jordan was as dramatic in its ending as it was at the beginning when an angel appeared to his father. He was imprisoned, and beheaded during Herod's birthday feast at the whim of Herod's illegal wife and her daughter, a dancing girl.

Feast day: 24 June (the old Midsummer Day) or 29 August.

Symbols: a camel-hair tunic; a locust; his head on a platter; a lamb; a lamb on a book with seven seals; an open Bible; a scroll with the words *Ecce Agnus Dei* ('Behold the Lamb of God').

Patron: of motorways, road construction workers, leather- and wool-workers.

St Joseph

Meaning: **from the Hebrew, 'may Jehovah increase'.**

Variations: Beppo, Jo, Joe, Joey

Female variations: Josephine, Fifi, Jo, Jolene, Josie, Josette, Pepita, Pepina

Little is known about St Joseph, the carpenter who was betrothed to Mary and became the earthly father of Jesus. Legend has it that he was an old man when he married Mary, who was already pregnant. He was reassured in a dream by an angel who proclaimed his betrothed's chastity. Certainly, the Gospels are silent about him, although the tradition that the marriage was never consummated is difficult to explain in the light of the brothers of Jesus mentioned later. What is not in contention, however, is the care he took both of mother and child and his obedience to God's will.

Feast day: 19 March.

Symbols: a carpenter's square, saw, axe and hatchet; a staff; a dove.

Patron: of carpenters, fathers, house-hunters, Austria, Belgium, Canada, Mexico, Peru and Vietnam.

Other St Josephs include Joseph of Arimathea, the devout Jew who offered his own expensive rock-tomb to shelter Jesus' body; he is thus patron saint of undertakers and cemetery staff. He has always had a place in English affections because of the legend that he came to Glastonbury after the Resurrection, bringing the chalice used at the Last Supper (Arthur's Holy Grail), and planting his staff, which grew into a flowering hawthorn tree. His symbols are a thorn tree, a box of ointment, a vase and the Holy Grail; his feast day is celebrated on 17 March.

A more disorderly but engaging St Joseph was the young Franciscan friar of Cupertino, Italy, who was only ordained by mistake, since he was thought to be mentally retarded. He may have been, but he was full of irrepressible joy and a strange ability to foretell events, which eventually persuaded the Church hierarchy that he was a saint. Rather more alarmingly, St Joseph became notorious for his astonishing habit of levitating, especially when moved by Christmas carols. Although this attracted many visitors, his superiors were not best pleased. He is now, appropriately enough, patron of astronauts and all involved in aviation. His feast day is 18 September.

St Julia

Meaning: **possibly from a Roman family name, meaning 'downy'.**

Female variations: **Gillian, Gill, Gillie, Jill, Jilly, Juliana, Jules, Julie, Juliet, Julitta**

St Julia of Corsica was a Christian from Carthaginia who was sold as a slave in 439. She was taken to Corsica by her master who was proud of her goodness and beauty, and found herself being coveted by Felix, the pagan governor. She refused to renounce her faith or her virginity, and was tortured and crucified.

Feast day: 22 May.

Symbols: a cross and ropes; a scourge; a dove.

Patron: of Corsica.

St Julian

Meaning: **possibly from a Roman family name, meaning 'downy'.**

Variations: Gillean, Julius, Jolyon, Jolyan, Jules

St Julian the Hospitaller is the patron of many churches, hospitals and charities in Europe because of the strange story about him in the medieval *Golden Legend* (drawn up by Jacob of Voraigne between 1255–1266, containing lives of saints and short treatises on Christian festivals). Julian was horrified to discover that it predicted that he would kill his parents, so he sent himself into exile. He eventually married, but his loving parents searched for and found him, only to be killed by him in a terrible mistake, just as the prediction had said.

Full of terrible remorse, Julian and his wife abandoned their castle and wealth, and set up a pilgrims' hospice and ferry on the banks of a dangerous river. Shortly before their deaths, Julian rowed an angel –

well-disguised as a poor, ill pilgrim – across the river. Before the angel disappeared, he assured Julian that God had seen his penitence and forgiven the murder. Julian is the patron of ferrymen and innkeepers, and also those who travel, particularly – for some reason – circus artistes. His feast day is 12 February.

St Justin & St Justina

Meaning: from the Latin, 'just'.

Female variation: Justine

Justin was one of the first Christian philosophers. He was born in 100, in Samaria, to a Greek-speaking family. Justin travelled to Alexandria, the great city of learning, where he studied many different philosophies but was eventually baptized a Christian. He wrote many treatises, some of which survive, and travelled to many countries, preaching the Gospel (as a layman), to pagans and Jews. On his second visit to Rome, he was denounced to the authorities and executed. Justin's symbols are quill pens and a sword, and he is remembered on 1 June, especially by philosophers.

Three centuries later, Justina was to prove that right-minded women could be equally brave. She was a beautiful pagan princess who was martyred on her way to join the Bishop of Padua. Legend has it that it was her knees which left two dents in the stones of the bridge there, as she knelt to pray for help during her arrest. Her symbol is a unicorn, the friend of virgins, and her feast is celebrated on 7 October.

K

St Kevin

Meaning: from Old Irish, 'handsome at birth'.

Variation: Kevan

St Kevin (or Coemgen) was a very attractive character – legends abound about how he loved and was beloved of birds and animals. Some legends can be found in Helen Waddell's book *Beasts and Saints* (Constable, 1934), but one tells of how he remained in prayer for so long that a blackbird nested in his hand. Kevin refused to move until she had hatched her brood and the fledglings were safely launched. St Kevin was born in Leinster and founded a monastery at Glendalough, County Wicklow, where he died in 618.

Feast day: 3 June.

Patron: of Ireland.

St Kieran

Meaning: **from Old Irish, 'black-haired'.**

Variations: Kerry

Female variations: Kerry, Ciara, Ciaran

St Kieran, or Ciaran, was another Irish saint. He was born in Co. Meath and was sent as a boy to become a monk in St Finnian's monastery. From there, he went to study under St Enda, and then left to found his own monastery at Clonmacnoise, Co. Offaly, which later became one of the greatest of Ireland's places of holiness and learning. He died in about 549; literally, just before his death, he seemed to be coming to life again – perhaps one of the earliest recorded near-death-experiences.

L

St Laurence

Meaning: from the Latin, 'of Laurentium' or 'a bay tree'.

Variations: Lanty, Larry, Laurie, Laurien, Lawrence, Lawrie, Lonnie, Lorrie

Female variations: Laurencia, Laura, Laurel, Lauren, Laurie, Loretta, Lori, Lorrie

Extraordinary stories are told of this third-century martyr, and traditional Catholics believe he is well-worth cultivating because he is thought to hold the privilege of rescuing a soul from purgatory every Fri-day. This was awarded to him in recognition of the par-ticularly horrible martyrdom he suffered, which was – among many other tortures – to be roasted to death on a gridiron.

Laurence was one of the seven deacons of Rome, appointed to serve the poor and needy; he also served Pope Sixtus II as his librarian. When Sixtus was arrest-ed and put to death in one of Emperor Valerian's perse-cutions, Laurence was commanded to hand over all the wealth of the Church. He asked for three days' grace, and then presented to the authorities a huge crowd of poor and handicapped people, widows and orphans, saying: 'Here is the Church's treasure.' This so annoyed the Roman authorities that Laurence was also arrested. The story goes that he never lost his serenity throughout the dreadful agonies to which he was subjected; as he was stretched out on the grid-iron his last words were: 'Turn me over, I'm cooked on this side.'

Feast day: 10 August.

Symbols: a dalmatic (the robe a deacon wears for Communion); a thurible or censer (container for burning incense); a gridiron; a plate of money.

Patron: of cooks, librarians and poor people; also Sri Lanka.

St Leo

Meaning: **from the Latin, 'Lion'.**

Variations: Leoline, Leon, Leonard, Lionel

Female variations: Leonora, Leonore, Leonie, Leonarda, Leona, Leonarda

Leo I was one of the greatest popes of the Church, being a learned theologican and an able, energetic and brave leader – for instance, he personally persuaded

Attila the Hun not to invade Rome in 452, and prevented a massacre when Genseric (King of the Vandals) and his men eventually succeeded in invading Rome in 455. It was Leo's *Tome* which finally squashed the monophysite heresy which was becoming popular at that time (that is, that Christ's earthly self was always of a divine nature and therefore could not really suffer or die).

Feast day: 11 April.

Symbols: a statue of Mary; a pick-axe; a horse; Attila kneeling.

St Leonard

Meaning: **from the Latin and Old German, 'lion bold'.**

Variations: Len, Lenard, Lennie, Lenny, Leo, Leon

Female variations: Leo, Leona, Leonarda

A popular medieval saint in France, Germany and Britain, little is known for sure about St Leonard. A book written about him in the eleventh century (*The Life of St Leonard*) recounts that he was a hermit who refused a bishopric and went to live in a forest in southern France. One day, King Clovis and his wife were riding through the forest when the queen, who was pregnant, unexpectedly went into labour. St Leonard gave them shelter and delivered the baby, and the king was so thankful that he granted him as much land as he could ride around on a donkey in one night, and a pardon for any prisoners he visited. Leonard built a monastery on the land he was granted, and many of the men freed by the royal pardon joined Leonard there. It is thought that his monastery also became a popular shrine for returning crusaders, especially those who had been taken prisoner and had invoked Leonard's aid for their release.

Feast day: 6 November.

Symbols: a chain with manacles; broken chains; a fountain.

Patron: of women in childbirth and prisoners, especially prisoners-of-war.

St Louis

Meaning: **from Old German, 'glorious battle'.**

Variations: Aloys, Aloysius, Lew, Lewes, Lewis, Lou, Louie, Ludovic, Luis

The meaning of 'Louis' has a certain irony in the case of St Louis, King Louis IX of France. Although he led two crusades, the first ended in defeat and his own capture, and the second caused his death from dysentery at Tunis in 1270. On the other hand, his efforts to drive the English from France were more successful and he managed to make a treaty with his brother-in-law,

Henry III. Louis was a man of great integrity, managing to balance the demands of kingship with his spiritual life as a Third Order Franciscan. It is well known that he had a particular distaste for bad language and would not tolerate it in those around him. He was happily married to Margaret of Provence, by whom he had eleven children. His greatest monument is the stunning Sainte-Chapelle in Paris, which was built to house a relic believed to have been the original crown of thorns.

Feast day: 25 August.

Symbols: a crown and sceptre tipped with the Hand of God; a fleur-de-lys; a dove.

Patron: of masons and sculptors.

St Louise

Female variations: Loise, Lois, Louie, Louisa, Lu, Luisa, Lulu

St Louise, a compatriot of King Louis but born 300 years later in 1591, was a wealthy young widow. Her confessor, St Vincent de Paul, saw potential in her for great spiritual development rather than mere charity, and Louise began to work with the poorest of Paris. Gradually, she attracted other women to her and she founded a new Order, the Daughters of Charity, 'whose convent is the sickroom, and whose cloister is the streets'. Their work spread throughout France, but it was their Hotel

Dieu in Paris which inspired Florence Nightingale to develop her own hospitals 300 years later.

Feast day: 15 March.

Patron: of widows, orphans and social workers.

St Lucy

Meaning: **from the Latin, 'light'.**

Variations: Lucian, Lucien, Lucius

Female variations: Lucasta, Lucia, Lucille, Lucinda, Lucinde

'Lucy' means 'light' and it may be for this reason that her feast day falls on the winter solstice. It may be, though, because legend has it that she plucked out her eyes and presented them on a plate to the man whose thwarted lust drove him to denounce her as a Christian. Whatever the truth of that story, it seems that Lucy was a beautiful young girl of Syracuse in Sicily, living in the third or fourth century. She accompanied her suffering mother to the shrine of St Agnes, where their prayers for a cure were answered. This miracle persuaded Lucy to consecrate her life to God and to give away all her wealth. Her fiancé betrayed her, and she was cruelly tortured and executed. Lucy is a greatly-loved saint of Sweden, and her feast day is celebrated with special food and processions of girls with wreaths of candles on their heads.

Feast day: 13 December.

Symbols: a lamp; a dagger; three crowns; two oxen; a cup; ropes.

Patron: of all who work with lights, glaziers, and those with eye trouble.

St Luke

Meaning: from the Greek, 'of Lucania' or 'wolf'.

Variations: Lucas, Luck

By tradition, Luke was a Greek-speaking Gentile, and besides writing the third Gospel, he was Paul's 'beloved physician' and also a painter. Although scholars now find as many Hebrew themes in the Gospel as Gentile ones, Luke's work is still characterized by its emphasis on the emotional, and its sympathy with women. Again, traditionally, Luke is believed to have painted Mary's portrait and recounted his version of the nativity from her own memories.

Feast day: 18 October.

Symbols: a winged ox; bottles of medicine; a book and pen; brushes and a palette; a picture of Mary.

Patron: of doctors, painters, butchers, glassmakers, goldsmiths, lacemakers and lawyers.

M

St Madeleine

Meaning: **from the Hebrew, 'of Magdala'.**

Female variations: Mad, Maddy, Madeline, Magda, Magdalene, Malina, Lena

Although there were three beatified Magdalenas and a St Magdalene (or Madeleine), the inspiration for this popular name was, of course, Mary of Magdala. There is great controversy as to whether or not she was the prostitute who anointed Jesus' feet (Luke 7:37–50) and/or Mary of Bethany. What is written of her is that she had 'seven devils', and that after her healing by Jesus she became one of his followers. Not only did she wait at the foot of the Cross with Mary and the other women, but it was she to whom the risen Christ appeared first; it was also to her that the news of the Resurrection was first entrusted. This meant that Mary Magdalene was often known as the 'first Apostle'. In the West, where she was believed to have been both the penitent prostitute and the contemplative Mary of Bethany, she became one of the most loved and revered saints of the Middle Ages.

Feast day: 22 July.

Symbols: fine clothes and loose hair; a pot of ointment; a skull; a vase; a crucifix.

Patron: of penitents, perfumiers, hairdressers, glovers and contemplatives.

St Margaret

Meaning: **from the Greek, 'a pearl'.**

Female variations: Daisy, Greta, Madge, Maggie, Maisie, Mamie, Margaretta, Margery, Marghanita, Margot, Marguerite, Marina, Marjorie, Marjory, May, Meg, Megan, Meghan, Peggy, Rita

Perhaps the most attractive St Margaret was the gentle and strong-willed English woman of noble birth who escaped to Scotland after William the Conqueror defeated the English royal house. She married Malcolm, the rather brutal King of Scotland, and bore him several children. Her personal influence affected the Scottish court for good, and she also persuaded the Church to conform to Western disciplines. She and her husband founded Dunfermline Abbey and one of her sons, David, was to become both a king and a saint. Her feast day is on 16 November and she is a patron of Scotland.

Better known is St Margaret of Antioch, although the legend of her martyrdom is probably a romantic tale, very similar to that of Catherine (qv Catherine, page 23). Her symbols are a chained dragon, a garland of pearls, a wreath of marguerites, a daisy, a sheep, a girdle, a cross and a crown. Her feast day is on 20 July, and she is patron of childbirth and nurses. St Margaret-Mary Alacoque is most well known among Catholics as the seventeenth-century French nun of the Visitation Order who had visions of Jesus showing his 'Sacred Heart'. She was directed to spread the practice of particular devotion to the 'Sacred Heart' which, after some opposition from her convent, she did. Her symbol is the Sacred Heart of Jesus, shown as a heart in flames, and her feast day is 17 October.

St Mark

Meaning: **from the Latin, 'of Mars' – the Roman god of war.**

Variations: Marc, Marcel, Marcus, Marius, Martin

Female variations: Marcella, Marceline, Marcia, Marsha, Martina

If the young man whose house was used for the Last Supper, and who – wrapped only in a sheet – stole after Jesus and his disciples to the Garden of Gethsemane is the author of Mark's Gospel, and also Paul's companion and Peter's amanuensis, we can build up a surprisingly full picture of St Mark. He was probably too young to have been allowed to join Jesus' followers, but was obviously drawn to this great teacher, to whom his mother had opened her house.

Despite his symbol being a winged lion, however, Mark was perhaps as nervous as the rest of us. As well as running away from the soldiers in the garden on that fateful night, leaving the only thing he was wearing in their hands, he abandoned Paul on his first missionary journey, being rather overwhelmed by it all. It took all the persuasion of his cousin Barnabas, who was with them, to reconcile Paul to Mark. Still, Mark did recover his courage – and it is a braver person who conquers fear than feels none – and joined Paul again. He accompanied him to Rome where he wrote what is probably the first Gospel. Most scholars believe that this was the memoir of Peter, although it has far more to it than that since it is so cleverly constructed to give the Gospel message 'between the lines'. We do not know what became of Mark after Peter and Paul were executed. It is said that he became Bishop of Alexandria and was martyred there, and that his body was moved to Venice in the ninth century.

Feast day: 25 April.

Symbols: a pen; a book and scroll; a winged lion; a scroll with the words *Pax tibi* ('Peace be to you').

Patron: of cattle farmers, lawyers, glaziers, and Venice.

St Martha

Meaning: **from the Hebrew, 'a lady'.**

Female variations: Marta, Martie, Marty

Martha is the patron saint of all those people who have little imagination and no great religious feeling, but who nevertheless get on with serving other people for the sake of Christ. When Jesus was staying with her family in Bethany, she complained to him that her sister Mary was doing nothing (apart from listening to Jesus) and that she, Martha, was having to do all the cooking on her own. Jesus was unimpressed. He was not about to banish Mary, who was listening so intently, to the kitchen. But it was for Martha that he undertook the dangerous journey back to Bethany when he heard that their brother, Lazarus, had died, and for her that he raised Lazarus from death. Their encounter – 'I am the resurrection and the life', 'I believe that thou art the Christ, the Son of God' – is one of the most moving in John's Gospel. It is a little Passion, prefiguring Jesus' own, and it is the sensible, grumpy Martha, not the saintly Mary, whose faith evokes Jesus' power.

Feast day: 29 July.

Symbols: a water pot and asperge; cooking pots; a ladle; a broom; a bunch of keys at her waist; a dragon bound with a girdle.

Patron: of housewives, cooks, waiters and dieticians.

St Martina & St Martin

Meaning: **from the Latin, 'of Mars' – the Roman god of war.**

Female variations: Marta, Martie, Martina, Tina

Women may be named after St Martina, a legendary Roman martyr, but it is more likely that they would be under the patronage of St Martin of Tours (born 315), who was one of the most popular saints of the Middle Ages. Many English churches are dedicated to this saint, and the name was given to boys and girls alike (as was common in medieval times), as well as to the bird.

The story most often recounted about Martin, a Hungarian soldier, concerns his time in the Roman army. One day, when he was stationed in Amiens, France, he met a beggar and having nothing to give him, he slashed his cloak in half and shared it with him. Later, Christ, wrapped in the half cloak, appeared to him in a dream and Martin was converted. He obtained a discharge from the army, not without difficulty, and became a hermit. He then became a monk under St Hilary, and eventually founded his own community.

He was not allowed to live peacefully as a religious for long, however, before the people of Tours insisted that he be consecrated as their bishop. Martin was even more horrified than the other bishops, who thought him rather too ascetic and unkempt to do honour to the position. He tried to run away but was betrayed by the loud honking of a goose that he disturbed. As a bishop, Martin continued to travel to the remotest places, preaching and working miracles. At his funeral procession (made up of 2000 monks) there was an outbreak of summer weather; today, good weather at about that time of year is called a 'St Martin's Summer'. His death coincided with the tasting of the new season's wine, so we also use the phrase 'Martin-drunk'.

Feast day: 11 November.

Symbols: a horse; a sword and a coat cut in half; a goose; a scourge; a hare; broken idols; a chair in flames; a demon at his feet.

Patron: of beggars, soldiers (especially cavalry), riders, tailors, drinkers and innkeepers.

St Mary

Meaning: **from the Hebrew, 'bitter'.**

Female variations: Maia, Maire, Mame, Mamie, Manon, Maria, Marian, Mariana, Marianne, Marice, Marie, Mariel, Marietta, Marilyn, Marion, Marisa, Maryanne, Masha, Maura, Maureen, May, Meriel, Meryl, Mimi, Minette, Minnie, Miriam, Mitzi, Moira, Moire, Mollie, Molly

Mary, the mother of Christ, is the most revered saint in the Christian world, and has several festivals in the Church's year. It is not surprising that her name has been one of the most popular for girls in all countries, as well as being used by boys in combination with a masculine name in Latin countries (like José Maria, for example). Mary also has various titles such as Maria de la Concepcion or Maria del Pilar, the title often being used as a name on its own – so you have girls named Pilar, Concepcion, Dolores, Consuela and Mercedes. The important quality of Mary was her willing obedience to Gabriel's announcement of the divine *fiat*. Her own *fiat* ('may it be unto me according unto Thy word') is often seen as the turning point when salvation came to the human race. She is also loved as the faithful woman who carried, bore and tended Jesus, and who witnessed his death and resurrection.

Principal feast days: 8 December, the (Immaculate) Conception; 25 March, the Annunciation; 31 May, the Visitation; 15 August, her Assumption into heaven; 8 September, her birthday.

Symbols: roses; lilies; the Christ-child.

Patron: of all women, especially mothers.

St Matilda

Meaning: **from Old German, 'battle strength'.**

Female variations: Mattie, Maud, Maude

Matilda was a German queen, the wife of Henry I and mother of Emperor Otto I, Henry 'the Quarrelsome', St Bruno, Archbishop of Cologne, and others. After the death of her husband, she lived for another 32 years at the mercy of Otto and Henry's unkindness. Her compassion for the poor and her devotion to the Church particularly annoyed them, but it earned her, at the very least, the love of her people.

Feast day: 14 March.

Symbols: a church and crucifix; a money bag; an altar.

St Matthew

Meaning: from the Hebrew, 'gift of Jehovah'.

Variations: Matt, Matthias

Female variations: Mattea, Matthea, Mattie, Matty

Surprisingly little is known about the man who gave us the longest of the synoptic Gospels. Matthew appears in the Gospels as a Jew who was collaborating with Romans as one of their tax collectors. Mark and Luke call him 'Levi' which meant that he belonged to the priestly tribe of Israel. Jesus' call to follow him must have surprised the other Jewish disciples, since 'good' Jews hated the collaborators, but he is said to have obeyed the call at once, leaving his ill-gotten gains for a rather more ascetic lifestyle. Tradition has it that Matthew was martyred in Ethiopia or Persia, and that his remains were brought to Brittany, France.

Feast day: 21 September.

Symbols: a money bag or a chest; a winged man; a dolphin; a scroll of his Gospel; a carpenter's square; an axe; pen and ink; a sword; stones.

Patron: of all who work with money, including, of course, taxmen and taxwomen.

St Maximilian

Meaning: **from the Latin, 'the greatest'.**

Variations: Max, Maxime, Maximus

Female variations: Maxine

The Second World War witnessed the death of many Christians, some of whom showed a depth of faith which still inspires people today. One of these was Maximilian Kolbe, who was executed in 1941 and canonized in 1983. Fr Maximilian Kolbe was a Polish Franciscan friar who became the head of a large friary at Niepokalonow. With great courage, the friars sheltered many refugees, many of whom were Jewish. Maximilian was arrested and taken to Auschwitz. He worked ceaselessly to encourage and support his fellow friars and the other prisoners, and when one was arbitrarily chosen to suffer death by starvation as a reprisal for another prisoner's escape, Fr Kolbe offered to take his place. He remained as cheerful and calm as ever for a fortnight, always encouraging the men who were suffering and dying alongside him. Eventually, the Nazis lost patience and gave him a lethal injection on 14 August.

Feast day: 14 August.

Patron: of all those who have become dependent on drugs.

St Melania

Meaning: from the Greek, 'black-haired'.

Female variations: Linda, Lynda, Mel, Mela, Melanie, Melinda, Melly, Melony

There were two St Melanias, known as 'the Elder' and 'the Younger' and they were related as grandmother and granddaughter. Melania the Elder took advantage of her very early widowhood to travel to Palestine and work with St Jerome in the 370s. She died in Jerusalem in 410, and her feast day is the 8 June. Her son obviously did not share his mother's spiritual ambitions for he insisted on marrying off his daughter, Melania the Younger, to a wealthy young cousin called Valerius Pinianus.

Melania's piety and compassion for the poor was an irritation to her family – especially her husband – but after the death of their two babies, he came round to her point of view. They sold much of their property and freed their slaves, much to their family's horror. When Rome was invaded by the Visigoths, however, they were free to escape to North Africa where Melania had other estates. Later, she and her husband moved to Palestine; after his death, Melania founded a convent on the Mount of Olives where she copied manuscripts until she died in 439. Although she found her grandmother rather a formidable woman, Melania came to know St Paulinus of Nola, St Augustine of Hippo and St Jerome, and they in turn thought very highly of her and her husband. Theirs is one of the happier stories of a Christian couple in the early Church.

Feast day: 31 December.

Symbols: a model of a church; an open purse.

St Michael

Meaning: **from the Hebrew, 'Who is like the Lord?'.**

Variations: Micah, Michel, Mick, Micky, Mike, Mischa, Mitch, Mitchell

Female variations: Michaela, Michele, Michelle, Micheline, Mickie

It may seem strange to venerate an archangel along with once-mortal saints, but although the feasts of Raphael and Gabriel were added during this century, Michael has always been a popular 'saint'. Very many churches are dedicated to him, especially those on hills, since a vision of him was seen on Monte Gargano in Italy, between 492 and 496. It is not only in the

Christian calendar that Michael is so important: he is also honoured by Jews and Muslims as one of God's greatest angels and captain of the heavenly host, continually fighting the Devil (or his human representatives). The association of Michael with fighting comes from the verses in Revelation 12:7–9 about the great war in heaven, but he is also considered to be a special protector of the sick in the Eastern Orthodox Church. There is a tradition which says that Michael receives dying souls and weighs them in his scales; hence his patronage of grocers.

Feast day: 29 September.

Symbols: a man in full armour and huge wings, often carrying a shield and scales.

Patron: of grocers and supermarket staff, soldiers, radiologists and the dying.

St Monica

Meaning: **unknown**.

Female variations: Mona, Monique

Monica, in these psychologically-aware days, has suffered a bad press. The woman who literally pursued her son to urge his conversion and baptism is often thought of nowadays as just another manipulative and domineering mother. In fact, she produced one of the most brilliant theologians and writers of the ancient or modern eras, whose autobiography speaks of her with great affection – so she must have done something right! The son, of course, was Augustine (354–430), who was born in Thagaste, North Africa, and who returned from his studies under St Ambrose in Italy to become the Bishop of Hippo in 396. Monica never saw his consecration, for she died at the Italian port of Ostia on their journey back to Africa. One of the most moving chapters of Augustine's *Confessions* records their almost ecstatic conversation about heaven together there, one night, looking over the sea. Monica died about five days later.

Feast day: 27 August.

Symbols: a monstrance; a veil or handkerchief; a book; a girdle; a staff.

Patron: of mothers.

St Mungo

Meaning: **from the Gaelic, 'darling'.**

Mungo, in fact, is the nickname of Bishop Kentigern, who is thought to have founded the church at Glasgow, and who died c. 612. There are stories of him being forced to flee to Wales, where he was able to found a monastery. St Asaph succeeded Kentigern as Abbot when he returned to Scotland by order of King Rederech, who was a Christian. No one knows the truth of all this, nor of the extraordinary miracles attributed to him, but the emblems of one of them – a ring and a fish – are on the heraldic arms of Glasgow city, of which he is patron. The story goes that the queen gave a ring, which had been her husband's present to her, to a knight of his court with whom she was in love. While the king and the knight were out hunting one day, they rested by a river. The knight fell asleep and the king noticed the ring on his finger. Suppressing his rage, he slipped the ring off and threw it into the river, saying nothing. When he returned home, however, he demanded the ring of his wife and when she could not produce it, ordered her execution. She could get no help from the knight, so she begged help from St Kentigern. He was filled with pity for her, since his own mother, a Pictish princess, had been seduced by Eugenius III, king of the Scots. So he prayed that the woman would be granted time for repentance. The ring was miraculously recovered from the belly of a salmon caught in the Clyde, and the queen lived to do penance and to become a faithful wife.

Feast day: 14 January.

Symbols: a ring and a fish.

N

St Natalia

Meaning: **from the Latin, 'the birth' (i.e. of Christ).**

Female variations: Natalie, Nathalia, Nathalie, Natasha, Natty, Nettie, Tasha

Two Natalias are venerated as martyrs, together with their husbands. Nothing much is known of the ninth-century Natalia and Aurelius, except that they were beheaded in Toledo during the Moorish persecutions. The earlier Natalia is thought, in fact, to have died in peace long after witnessing the cruel execution of Adrian, her husband. He was one of the pagan officers in Nicomedia, and was so impressed by the courage of the Christian prisoners in his charge that he became a Christian himself, inevitably ending up in his own jail. Natalia did all she could to alleviate the Christians' sufferings, but she could not prevent their deaths at the stake. A great storm quenched the fires before the bodies were burned, and Natalia – along with some of the Christian community – took the remains of these martyrs to be buried at Argyropolis. She remained there until her death, when she was buried alongside them.

Feast day: 8 September.

Symbols: an anvil; a lion; a tomb.

St Nathaniel

Meaning: **from the Hebrew, 'God has given'.**

Variations: Nat, Nathan, Nathaneal, Natty

See St Bartholomew, page 16.

St Nicholas

Meaning: **from the Greek, 'Victory of the people'.**

Variations: Claus, Cole, Colet, Colin, Nick, Nicky, Nichol

Female variations: Nicola, Nicole, Nicolette, Colette

St Nicholas is one of the most popular saints, as can be seen by the number of other saints who share his name, and the many variants of it for both boys and girls. He is, of course, better known as Father Christmas or Santa Claus. In many northern European countries, he fills shoes or stockings on 6 December, rather than on Christmas Eve.

We only know for certain that he was the bishop of Myra, in Asia Minor, in the fourth century. The popular legend that he saved three sisters from spinsterhood (or worse) by throwing three bags of gold through their windows, thus rendering them rich and marriageable, made the link with an anonymous bringer of presents. Apparently, a picture of this story was so confusing that it was understood to be Nicholas bringing back to life three children who had been murdered and hidden in a pickle tub, so the bishop developed a reputation for being especially fond of children. He was also credited with the rescue of shipwrecked sailors and three prisoners condemned to death.

Brewer's *Dictionary of Phrase and Fable* suggests that the reason 'the Knights of St Nicholas' is another name for thieves is not because Nicholas aids and abets them, but because he once induced some to give back what they had stolen. It is also reassuring to know that 'Old Nick' as a name for the Devil has nothing to do with the good bishop, but comes from 'Nick' – a Scandinavian evil spirit.

Feast day: 6 December.

Symbols: three golden apples on a book; three purses; three loaves; three golden apples; an anchor; a ship; a Trinity symbol on a cope (ceremonial cloak).

Patron: of children (especially boys), sailors, pawnbrokers, merchants, captives, Russia, and many other places and churches.

St Olivia & St Oliver

Meaning: **from the Latin, 'olive tree'.**

Variations: Ollie, Noll

Female variations: Liva, Livia, Livy, Nola, Nollie, Olive, Olivette, Ollie, Olva

No one is sure if the story of the beautiful Christian girl from Palermo who was carried away by pirates to Tunis is true. Once there, she lived the life of a hermit, but so many Muslims were converted by her example of holiness and her power to work miracles that the authorities tortured and executed her. What is certain is that she is, perhaps oddly, venerated among Muslims at Tunis even today, and the mosque of the city is called 'Temple of Olive'. Her feast day is 10 June and she is often portrayed in art with a brazier and leaden ropes.

Oliver Plunket was the last Catholic martyr to be hung, drawn and quartered at Tyburn in 1681. He was born in Ireland in 1629 and became Bishop of Armargh at the age of 40. He set about reforming the Church while trying to maintain good relations with the Protestant bishops but the political troubles in Ireland overwhelmed Christian principles. He was betrayed, tried and released, and then tried again – this time in London – where a corrupt court found him guilty and sentenced him to death. His feast day is 11 July.

P

St Patrick

Meaning: from the Latin, 'of the noble patrician class'.

Variations: Paddie, Paddy, Padraic, Padraig, Pat, Patrice

Female variations: Paddie, Pat, Patrice, Patricia, Patsy, Pattie, Tricia, Trish, Trisha

St Patrick has become synonymous with Ireland, the land to which he came as a missionary bishop in 432. It is rather surprising considering that Patrick was not Irish but a Romano-Briton, and his first experience of Ireland was as a slave, when he was captured and sold into slavery for about six years. After escaping to France and being consecrated by St Germanus in Auxerre, Patrick returned to Ireland where he travelled about, teaching and working miracles, as well as writing.

One of his best-loved traits was that of teaching the truths of the faith using homely, simple images; his example of the shamrock (or cloverleaf) representing the mystery of the Trinity has become universal, as well as his own personal symbol. He founded the great church at Armargh in 444 (where Oliver Plunket became bishop over 1000 years later), and died in 461.

Feast day: 17 March.

Symbols: an archbishop's cross; a shamrock; an Irish harp; fire; a font; a mitre; a dragon; a long staff; a wallet.

Patron: of Ireland and Nigeria.

St Paul

Meaning: from the Latin, 'small'.

Variation: Paulinus

St Paul needs no introduction. He was the apostle who first took the Gospel to the Gentile world, and who wrote many of the letters which make up the New Testament. He is also one of the apostles Luke writes about in Acts, and is believed to have been martyred in Rome during Nero's persecution of Christians, around 68. Many other St Pauls have followed, from Cyprus, Italy, Japan, Korea and even Roman Britain. The original St Paul seems to have been intellectually brilliant, something of a mystic, an indefatigable traveller and, at times, hot tempered.

Feast day: 29 June or 25 January.

Symbols: book and sword; serpent and fire; a palm tree; three fountains; a phoenix; scrolls with the names of his epistles.

Patron: of tentmaking (his own trade) and upholsterers.

St Paula

Female variations: Pauline, Paulette

St Paula of Bethlehem (347–404) was a Roman noble-woman who married and had five children. When her husband died, she became a disciple of St Jerome, and, with her daughter, St Eustochium, founded a convent and a pilgrim's hospice in Bethlehem. By all accounts, she was also intellectually gifted, learning both Greek and Hebrew, and studying the Bible. Jerome's letters praise her practical efficiency and her diplomacy, but are concerned about her excessive self-discipline and generosity to others. There is another St Paula of the nineteenth century, three other beatified Paulas, and a Blessed Pauline, a German woman who founded the Sisters of Christian Charity in 1849.

Feast day: 26 January.

Symbols: instruments of the Passion; a book and staff; a sponge; a scourge.

Patron: of widows.

St Peter

Meaning: **from the Greek, 'a stone'.**

Variations: Parry, Pearce, Perkin, Perry, Pete, Pierce, Piers, Pyrs

Female variations: Peta, Petra, Piera, Petrina, Pierina

Peter was, of course, pre-eminent among the apostles, being not only one of the inner circle of three (together with his brothers James and John), but also the disciple to whom Jesus entrusted the Church: 'You are a rock (*Petrus*): on you I will found my Church' (John 21:15).

From the Gospels, we have a picture of a fisherman who lived with his wife in Galilee and fished with his brother, Andrew, until they were called by Jesus to become 'fishers of men'. He was the apostle who denied his master three times on the night of Jesus' betrayal, and yet he was the man whom the risen Jesus told to 'feed my lambs'. He travelled to Rome where he became the leader of the Church, and it is thought that he dictated his memories to Mark, forming the first Gospel. And it was there that he faced execution, together with Paul, in about 67. There are legends of him travelling to Antioch with his wife and daughter, Petronilla (whose name, incidentally, is not derived from 'Peter', as many think, but from the Latin, Petronius) – but these are probably legendary.

Feast day: 29 June.

Symbols: two crossed keys; a crowing cock; a fish; two swords; a shepherd's staff and two keys.

Patron: of fishermen, boatbuilders and clockmakers.

St Philip

Meaning: **from the Greek, 'a lover of horses'.**

Variations: Phil, Pip

Female variations: Philippa, Phili, Pippa, Pippi

Philip was another of the 12 disciples, a respectably married Jewish fisherman from Galilee until he was called to follow Jesus. We know much less about him than Peter, but he was one of the disciples at the feeding of the 5000, so bread has become one of his symbols in art. He was also the apostle who converted Queen Candace's eunuch as he travelled back to Egypt after the Resurrection. Tradition has it that he went to Phrygia and was martyred at Hieropolis, but this is not known for certain.

Feast day: 3 May.

Symbols: a basket; three loaves and a cross; a carpenter's square; a patriarchal cross and spear.

Patron: of Luxembourg and Uruguay.

Q

St Quentin

Meaning: **from the Latin, 'a fifth child' or after the Roman tribe of the Quintii.**

Variations: Quinn, Quint, Quintin, Quinton

Female variations: Quinta, Quintilla

St Quentin was martyred sometime around 300 in the French town that bears his name, although nothing certain about him is known. Some think that he was the son of a Roman senator and was an officer in the Roman army before forsaking his wealth and position to become a missionary to Gaul. The symbols associated with him all refer to the many tortures he was said to have suffered but why he is patron of bombadiers, chaplains, locksmiths, tailors and porters is a mystery. Perhaps he should be a patron of all prisoners, for it is said that he was once released from prison by an angel.

Feast day: 31 October.

Symbols: a broken wheel; iron spits; a saltire cross (X).

R

St Raymond

Meaning: **from the Old German, 'strong or wise defence'.**

Variations: Ray, Raymund

Female variations: Raymonda, Raymonde

St Raymond of Penafort and St Peter Nolasco co-founded the Order of Our Lady of Ransom or the 'Mercedarians' in the early thirteenth century. This was a Spanish Order dedicated to rescuing Christians who had been taken prisoner by the Moorish occupation. St Raymond Nonnatus joined the Order and went to Algeria with ransom money for prisoners. When the money ran out, he offered himself in exchange for another man. This was agreed, but the Moors had not perhaps reckoned with Raymond's determination to preach the Gospel, even in their own territory. Threatened by the flow of converts and determined to stop him, they found an effective but crude method: they put a padlock through his lips and put him into prison. His guards were either kinder or greedier. They kept Raymond alive, at any rate, until he was himself ransomed by the Order and was able to make the journey home, where he died in 1240. His nickname means 'not born', which refers to the story that his mother died in childbirth. Raymond was delivered from her body by a doctor, and he is thought to have a special concern for 'all women labouring of child'.

Feast day: 31 August.

Symbols: a padlock; three or four crowns; a crown of thorns.

Patron: of pregnant women and babies, midwives and obstetricians, and Catalonia.

St Richard

Meaning: from Old English, 'a strong ruler'.

Variations: Dick, Dickie, Dickon, Richie, Rick, Ricky, Ritchie

Female variations: Richarda, Richenda, Rickie, Ricky

To drop the chalice during Communion must be every priest's nightmare, but St Richard of Chichester once did and apparently he miraculously did not spill a drop. Richard was born in 1197 and studied at Oxford, Paris and Bologna. He became the Chancellor of Oxford University, and later served as chancellor to St Edmund of Abingdon, who was then the Archbishop of

Canterbury. Trouble began when St Boniface of Mainz and King Henry III quarrelled over the right of appointment to the See of Chichester. Boniface appointed Richard, known to be a strong-minded and ascetic pastor as well as a scholar, whereas Henry had his own favourite, one of his own court who was, nevertheless, 'deficient in learning'. Richard had to wait for two years before the Pope upheld his claim, but once he took possession of his See, he proved to be a very effective and much-loved bishop.

Feast day: 3 April.

Symbols: a plough; a book and staff; a chalice at his feet.

Patron: of coach drivers.

St Robert

Meaning: **from Old German, 'bright fame'.**

Variations: Bert, Bertie, Bob, Bobbie, Rab, Rabbie, Rob, Robbie, Robby, Robin, Rupert

Female variations: Bobbie, Robbie, Robena, Roberta, Robin, Robina, Ruperta

There is a melancholy list of Roberts among the English Catholic martyrs of the Reformation, of whom the poet Robert Southwell is the most famous, but there are the happier lives of St Robert of Molesme and St Robert Bellarmine to recount.

St Robert of Molesme was an eleventh-century monk who founded a monastery in Burgundy at Molesme, but who eventually became one of the co-founders of the great Cistertian monastery at Citeaux. He was the Abbot there for 18 months, but then returned to Molesme, where he ruled as Abbot until his death at the age of 84. His feast is celebrated on 29 April.

Robert Bellarmine was one of the greatest Jesuit scholars of the Renaissance, and may take some credit for being sympathetic to (although not completely persuaded by) Galileo during the scientist's persecution by the Church. His feast day is 17 September, and he is patron of all ecclesiastical lawyers and catechists.

St Rock

Meaning: from Old German, 'crow' or
Old English, 'rock'.

Although the film star Rock Hudson is the first person of this name to spring to mind among English speakers, St Rock (or Roch) was well known and loved in France and Italy as a healer of disease, especially contagious diseases. He was born in 1293 to the wealthy governor of Montpellier. His parents died when he was still a young man, and Rock gave away all his wealth, in order to become a pilgrim. On his way to Rome, he healed many people of the plague which was then raging in Italy, until he himself became infected. He went into the forest to die, but was cared for by a dog who brought him food, and there the saint recovered. Rock returned to Montpellier so starved and looking so ill that none of his family recognized him and he was arrested as an imposter. For five years he lay in prison. When he died, it was discovered that he had the same birthmark as the infant Rock: the mark of a cross on his chest.

Feast day: 16 August.

Symbol: a dog.

Patron: of healers, prisoners and dog-owners.

St Rose

Meaning: **from Old German, 'horse' or from the Latin, 'rose'.**

Female variations: Rhoda, Rois, Rosa, Rosetta, Rosie, Rosina, Rosita, Rosy

St Rose of Lima (1586–1617) was the first American-born person to be canonized, although she was the daughter of Spanish parents who had come to settle in Peru. She was born in Lima, and became a Dominican Tertiary at the age of 20. Although she led an outwardly simple life, growing flowers and doing embroidery in order to help the family's finances, Rose inflicted terrible tortures on herself for fear of vanity, and seemed to endure strange mystical experiences which were investigated by the Church. Nowadays these are often considered to be signs of psychiatric disorder rather than holiness. Nevertheless, Rose was canonized not for these self-destructive traits but for her sympathy for the poor and slaves, the sick and the Peruvian Indians.

Feast day: 30 August.

Symbols: a crown of roses and thorns; a needle and thimble; a spiked crown.

Patron: of florists and gardeners, Latin America, the Philippines and Peru.

St Rupert

Meaning: from Old German, 'bright fame'.

Female variation: Ruperta

One St Rupert (together with his mother, St Bertha), lived as a hermit on the Rupertsburg near Bingen in the ninth century, and became particularly well-loved by the much more famous Hildegard of Bingen when she was Abbess there 300 years later. Another St Rupert who has been particularly popular in Ireland was the bishop of Worms, a Frenchman of the seventh century. He later became a missionary to Bavaria, and then to Austria.

Feast day: 27 March.

Symbols: a salt box; a model of a church; a basket of eggs.

S

St Simon

Meaning: **from the Hebrew, 'listening' or from the Greek. 'snub-nosed'.**

Variations: Si, Sim, Simeon

Female variation: Simone

As one of the Twelve, Simon the Zealot is one of the foremost saints in the Christian calendar; as one of the most anonymous, nothing much is known about him. The nickname 'Zealot' suggests that he was one of the underground Jewish freedom fighters who risked death by crucifixion for their terrorist warfare against the occupying Roman forces. Some traditions say that after the Resurrection he went to Egypt and Persia and was later martyred, and he is often venerated together with St Jude. Their feast day is 28 October, and Simon is often portrayed with the symbols of a fish and book, two fishes, an oar, a ship or a fuller's bat.

An English saint, Simon Stock, was born in Kent in 1165, and became the prior general of the Carmelites. Under his able leadership, four new houses were opened in the great medieval university cities of Oxford, Cambridge, Paris and Bologna. Carmelites wear a scapular – a long, sleeveless tunic put on over the habit – and Simon once had a vision of Mary who told him that no one who wore the scapular would ever go to Hell. This is the origin of the widespread sale of tiny token scapulars often worn by Roman Catholics – but whether this is quite what Mary had in mind is not clear. St Simon died in 1265 at Bordeaux but his body was brought back to be buried in Aylesford in Kent.

Feast day: 16 May.

Patron: of leatherworkers.

St Sophia

Meaning: **from the Greek, 'wisdom'.**

Female variations: Sonia, Sonnie, Sonya, Sophie

Although Sophia has become a very popular name, the saints who bore it are generally forgotten or legendary, like the martyr who is supposed to have been the mother of St Faith and her sisters. Perhaps it is the meaning of the name, 'wisdom', which has brought it back into fashion, or maybe it is just the current craze for Victorian girls' names.

Feast day: 30 September.

St Stephen

Meaning: **from the Greek, 'crowned'.**

Variations: **Etienne, Steffan, Stephan, Steve, Steven, Stevie**

Female variations: **Stephanie, Steffie, Steph, Stephana, Steve, Stevie**

St Stephen is of course, in the words of 'Good King Wenceslas'. The story of his death is written in Acts 6–7, and it tells of how Stephen, who had been chosen by the apostles to be the head of the band of seven deacons, 'did great wonders and miracles' and became a powerful preacher.

The angry Jews who were affronted by the claims of the disciples accused him of blasphemy and, according to Jewish law, stoned Stephen to death. Before he died, he apparently addressed the crowd with the sermon recorded in Acts (which is, indeed, stirring stuff!); as he finished, he exclaimed in wonder at the vision he had: 'I see the heavens opened, and the Son of Man standing at the right hand of God.' Like his Lord, Stephen gave his soul to God as he died, and prayed that his executioners would not be found guilty of their sin.

Feast day: 26 December.

Symbols: a dalmatic (a tunic-like vestment); three stones; stones in a napkin; stones on a book.

Patron: of stonemasons, builders and horses.

St Susanna

Meaning: **from the Hebrew, 'graceful white lily'.**

Female variations: Shushana, Susan, Sosanna, Sue, Sukey, Suki, Susanne, Susie, Suzanna, Suzanne, Suzette, Suzi, Zsa Zsa

One St Susanna may have been the beautiful niece of St Caius, Bishop of Rome, who was sought after by the Emperor Diocletian's friend, Maximian. When she refused him, she, her father and two uncles were all executed. Whatever the truth of the story, there was a Susanna who was martyred and buried in Rome. The popularity of this name in Britain is probably due more to the heroine in the apocryphal story of Tobit, but there are several saints called Susanna, including another martyr from Armenia who married a Russian prince from Georgia and who was killed by Persians in 473.

Feast day: 11 August.

Symbols: a crown at her feet, a sword.

T

St Teresa

Meaning: **from the Greek, 'of Tharasia' or 'reaper'.**

Female variations: Terese, Terrie, Terry, Tess, Tessa, Theresa, Therese, Tracey, Tracy

St Teresa of Avila and St Thérèse of Lisieux are two of the most extraordinary women of the Church, and both of them were quite different.

Teresa was a witty, energetic woman of the world who nevertheless became one of the greatest contemplatives. She worked with St John of the Cross and others to reform the Carmelite Order in which she had become professed as a nun. She lived during the time of the Counter-Reformation in Spain when there was a great flowering of learning and discipline in the Roman Catholic Church amidst the careless laxity of many of the clergy and religious houses. Certainly, much of that is to Teresa's credit, and she was the first woman to be honoured as a 'Doctor of the Church' for all her writings on prayer and the inner life.

Conversely, her letters and the descriptions of her that survive show us a fascinatingly contradictory saint who was impatient with 'stupid nuns' and yet humble about her own intellectual abilities; an ecstatic visionary who distrusted the supernatural phenomena which occurred around her; a brilliant cook; and someone who was determined to lead those who would follow her into a life of strict austerity and discipline.

Feast day: 15 October.

Symbols: roses and lilies; a heart in flames; flaming arrows; a dove.

Patron: of Spain.

Thérèse, by contrast, was a young and simple nineteenth-century Frenchwoman, who died of tuberculosis at the age of 24. Opinions about her differ: to many thousands, her autobiography, *Histoire d'une âme*, is a work of spiritual genius in its simplicity, humility and ordinariness. (She is patron of missionaries and pilots because she would offer to God, on their behalf, the few painful steps she was able to make each day during her illness.) Her powers of intercession were and are believed to be miraculous, and the shrine at Lisieux is one of the largest in the Roman Catholic Church. To others, the 'Little Flower' – as she liked to call herself – was a nauseating product of a rather febrile kind of French spirituality.

St Teresa and St Thérèse speak to different kinds of people, but they both experienced the love of God intensely, and could communicate the depths of their experience to others – that, not their brand of spirituality, is what matters.

Feast day: 3 October.

Symbols: flowers.

Patron: of florists, missionaries, airline pilots and France.

St Thomas

Meaning: **from the Aramaic, 'a twin'.**

Variations: Tam, Tamas, Tom, Tomas, Tompkin, Tommy

Female variations: Tamsin, Tamasine, Thomasina, Tammy, Tamara

Many St Thomases take their name from the apostle who is often called 'Doubting Thomas' from the story in John's Gospel (John 20:24–8). John also recalls him as the apostle of the heroic or fatalistic comment in 11:16 – 'Let us also go, that we may die with him' – when Jesus was preparing to go to Bethany, where Lazarus had died. It is also John who calls him 'Didymus' or 'the twin', although we do not know who his twin was. Thomas' recognition of the risen Christ ('My Lord and my God!' John 20:28) has become a powerful meditation prayer for many Christians. That is as much as we know of Thomas, the apostle, although a much later book called *The Acts of Thomas* (written in the second and fourth centuries by members of sects, such as the Gnostics) describes his founding of the church in Kerala in Southern India.

Feast day: 21 December.

Symbols: spear and lance: carpenter's square and lance; builder's rule; the five wounds of Christ; the Virgin Mary's girdle; a book and spear.

Patron: of architects, builders, carpenters, masons and surveyors.

Thomas à Becket (1118–1170), the statesman and archbishop of Canterbury who was murdered by Henry II, was the most important English saint in the Middle Ages, and his shrine became the most important centre for pilgrims after Rome and Santiago de Compostela. Although he was clearly similar to a politician in his obstinacy and ambition, he took his consecration as archbishop very seriously, and became known for his devotion, austerity and defence of the Church against the King. His help is invoked for blindness.

Thomas More (1478–1535), who was beheaded by Henry VIII, also refused to compromise his Christian beliefs for political expediency. He is another English saint loved for his wide learning and humanity. He is the patron of civil servants and lawyers. The other very well-known St Thomas is, of course, the great theologian, St Thomas Aquinas (1225–1274), whose symbol is a star, and who was, himself, the star of medieval science, theology and prayer. Naturally, he is the patron of scholars, especially theologians. It is reasonable, therefore, that he should also be the patron of all pencil makers.

St Timothy

Meaning: **from the Greek, 'honour to God'.**

Variations: Tim, Timmie, Timmy

Female variation: Timothea

St Paul writes to Timothy with such obvious and avun-
cular affection that it is hard not to feel it too, although
we know only a little about him. Indeed, Paul ends his
second letter to Timothy with a moving appeal for his
company. From Acts and Paul's letters we know that
he was Jewish through his mother, Eunice, but had a
Greek father. Although Eunice and her mother, Lois,
were Christians and had brought Timothy up as a
Christian too, Paul himself gave Timothy instruction in
the faith, and also circumcised him, in order to show
the Jewish Christians that Christianity was not radi-
cally anti-Jewish, but a fulfilment of everything they
believed in. Later, Timothy was given charge over the
Church at Ephesus and is thought to have been its first
bishop. Some say that he was beaten to death for his
opposition to the pagan festivities in honour of their
goddess and great tourist attraction, Diana.

Feast day: 24 January.

Symbols: a club and stones; a broken image of the
goddess Diana.

Patron: of people with digestive disorders ('Take a little
wine for thy stomach's sake,' Paul tells him).

u

St Ursula

Meaning: from the Latin, 'little bear'.

Variation: Orson

Female variation: Orsa, Ulia, Ursa, Ursulina

Apparently, Ursula was a British princess who refused to marry a pagan suitor until, playing for time, she had made a pilgrimage to Rome with 11,000 virgins. The required companions were eventually found and Ursula set off with her entourage to Rome, where she met the Pope. She was assured in a dream that she would be martyred on the return journey and would therefore avoid the threat of marriage; she told this to the Pope who, also keen for martyrdom, then joined her. When they reached Cologne on the return journey, they met the pagan suitor who was now converted and also anxious for martyrdom, and there were some Huns who were happy to oblige. Historians believe that some women seem to have been martyred at Cologne before the late fourth century, so maybe this story has a high degree of truth in it. Sadly, Ursula is no longer on the official Roman calendar, but she has given her name to an Order of nuns, as well as many other women, and she and her companions are immortalized as 'the eleven who went up to heaven' in some interpretations of the song, 'Green grow the rushes-O'.

Feast day: 21 October.

Symbols: an ermine-lined cloak; two arrows; a dove; a ship; a crown.

Patron: of women, girls and teachers.

V

St Valeric

Meaning: **from the Latin, 'strong' or from the Roman family name, Valerius.**

Variations: Valerian, Valery

Female variations: Val, Valeria

The most common use of 'Valerie' for English speakers is as a girl's name, and must refer back to St Valeria, who was supposed to have been the wife of St Vitalis, and the mother of St Gervase and St Protase. She and her husband are honoured as martyrs, although nothing is known for certain about them. Her symbol is a severed head, and her feast day is celebrated on 28 April.

In France, however, it is St Walaricus, or St Valéry, who is honoured. Walaricus was a fifth-century monk who began his religious life at Luxeuil and then set out as a missionary to northern France. He later settled down and became an abbot at Leuconaus; he died in 620. It is said that he was specially invoked by William the Conqueror who wanted fair winds for his foray into England in 1066. Perhaps his obviously efficient intervention in this matter explains why he is still so well thought of on the other side of the English Channel, and so obscure to the English. He is remembered on April Fools' Day.

St Veronica

Meaning: from the Latin, 'a true icon'.

Female variations: Nicky, Ronnie, Vera, Verena, Veronique

'Veronica' is an anagram of *'vera icon'* or 'true image' and the name has become associated with the story of the woman of Jerusalem who stopped Jesus on his way to crucifixion and wiped his bloody, perspiring face with her handkerchief. As a miraculous reward for her compassion, Jesus' features were imprinted on the cloth, which is kept as a precious relic in St Peter's, Rome. Some people believe that Veronica was also the woman with the 'issue of blood' whom Jesus healed, others that the liturgical veil called the 'vernicle' eventually became personified as a woman called Veronica. However it may be, Veronica herself has become a true image of compassion in her own right, and a beautiful picture in the otherwise brutal story of the Crucifixion.

Feast day: 12 July.

Symbols: Christ's face printed upon a veil.

Patron: of laundry workers.

St Victor

Meaning: from the Latin, 'victory'.

Variations: Vic, Vick, Victor

There is a second-century martyr named Victor, who was a soldier in the Roman army, and supposed to have been beheaded in Milan in 303. Another Victor, of Marseilles (also a soldier in that army), became a Christian and was martyred sometime during the third century. Little is known about him, but the tradition is that he underwent the most frightful tortures, being strengthened by the presence of Christ and hosts of angels. When he was taken to bow down before pagan gods, Victor merely kicked them over, and had his foot cut off before he was finally beheaded. These Victors are remembered on 8 May and 21 July respectively.

St Victoria

Female variations: Vicki, Vickie, Vicky, Victorine, Vita

There were three women named Victoria martyred in the early Church. One was an African girl who ran away with several other Christians and who chose death with them rather than marriage to a pagan or making a plea of insanity. Another was martyred with her sister, Anatolia, in Italy, and another was killed with her husband, Acisclus, in Spain. Their feast days are 11 February, 23 December and 17 November.

St Vincent

Meaning: **from the Latin, 'conquering'.**

Variations: Vin, Vince, Vincente, Vinny

Female variation: Vincentia

Both of the St Vincents who are still well known lived up to their name. The first, St Vincent of Lerins, was a great theologian who retired to the tiny island off Cannes and yet whose work on the Trinity shaped the Church's self-understanding even to this day. He was one of the great writers who conquered the Arian heresy – contemporary with St Athanasius – and, indeed, many people believe that he wrote what we call the 'Athanasian' creed. He also gave a usefully elastic definition of what is catholic truth: that is, that it must always have been held to be true, 'always, everywhere, and by all the faithful'. This definition is still used in ecclesiastical arguments today. His feast day is 24 May.

The enemy of St Vincent de Paul was not so much a theological heresy as a materialistic streak, so it is a remarkable thing that he has become synonymous, in France at least, with the care and service of the poor. Born in 1580, of very poor parents, Vincent seemed to be a 'career priest' in the corrupt atmosphere of aristocratic France. What changed his heart may have been his experience of living and working with people who lived in great luxury side by side with others in extreme poverty. Or it may have been the influence of Fr Berulle and Madame de Gondi who were working in Paris. Whatever caused him to do it, Vincent founded an Order dedicated to helping the most destitute in society, and encouraged St Louise de Marillac to begin a similar order for women, the Sisters of Charity. He even took the place of a galley-slave for some months, ruining his own health, in order to restore the slave to his family. Throughout his life, he managed to continue his friendship with the rich and influential, even the French Queen, Anne of Austria. He encouraged them to use their position to help the poor, while giving himself unreservedly to the most helpless in society.

Feast day: 27 September.

Symbols: a model of an orphanage or hospital; a child in his arms.

Patron: of all charities, hospitals and prisons, and Madagascar.

W

St William

Meaning: **from Old German, 'helmet of resolution'.**

Variations: Bill, Billie, Billy, Gwylim, Liam, Will, Willie, Willis, Willy, Wilmot, Wilson

Female variations: Billie, Billy, Min, Mina, Minna, Minnie, Valma, Velma, Wilhelmina, Vilette, Vilma, Wilella, Wilhelmine, Willa, Willamina, Wilma, Wilmette, Wilmot, Wylma

William is such a popular name both in England and in France that it is hardly surprising that there are many listed in the calendar of saints, as well as a sad roll of beatified men who were tortured and executed during the Reformation in England. It is difficult to choose any one of them rather than another, but St William of Gellone seems to have been an attractive character, simply because he combined outward 'masculine' virtues in order to be the ideal Christian knight, with more inward qualities that led him to found an abbey near Aniane, to which he retired as a monk. He is remembered on 28 May.

St William of York was also rather an interesting mixture of the pragmatic and spiritual. He was appointed as Bishop of York in 1140, but there was a great deal of fuss because his enemies accused him of simony (buying or selling Church appointments) and sexual laxity. Pope Innocent II upheld his cause and he was consecrated, but seven years later he was deposed by Pope Eugenius III, on the advice of St Bernard of Clairvaux among others. He must have had redeeming qualities, however, for after spending some years in ascetic seclusion, Pope Anastasius IV restored him to his See, to the joy of his flock. His feast day is 8 June.

St Winifred

Meaning: from Old German, 'peaceful friend' or Old Welsh, 'blessed reconciliation'.

Female variations: Freda, Fredi, Freddie, Gwenfrewi, Win, Winnie, Winny, Wyn, Wynne

There were many springs associated with healing in medieval Britain, often the origin of a town or village, and often called Holywell or having the suffix 'well'. Holywell in North Wales grew up on the spot where Winifred (Gwenfrewi) was beheaded by the furious and frustrated Caradog of Hawarden, who had wanted to marry this chaste Christian girl. Her uncle, St Beuno, calmly replaced Winifred's head and thus restored her to life, and Caradog was swallowed up by the earth beneath his feet. Winifred became a nun and died at Gwytherin about 650. The spring became a place of pilgrimage for over 1000 years.

Feast day: 3 November.

Symbols: a shepherd's staff; a sword.

Z

St Zachary

Meaning: **from the Hebrew, 'the Lord has remembered'.**

Variations: Zacchaeus, Zacharias, Zachariah, Zack, Zacky, Zak, Zechariah, Zeke

The story of Zachariah (or 'Zachary' in its popular English form) at the beginning of Luke's Gospel forms a diptych with that of Joseph. He was the father of Jesus' cousin, John the Baptist, and occasionally served as a priest in the temple. An angel appeared to him while he was performing his priestly tasks to announce the conception of John by his wife, Elizabeth, although she was elderly and barren. Zachariah, like his counterpart Joseph, was incredulous at first; so much so that he was silenced for his unbelief. This lasted until the child was born and he had corroborated his wife's obedient decision to name her promised child John, as the angel had directed. If Zachariah was initially faithless, he did eventually catch on. Like 'Doubting Thomas', Zachariah might be a special patron of the cynical and slow.

Feast day: 5 November.

Symbols: a thurible; a priest's vestments; an altar; an angel; a lighted candle.

St Zoe

Meaning: **from the Greek, 'life'; used to translate 'Eve' from the Hebrew into Greek.**

Another martyr of the early Church, Zoe was married to a slave called Hesperus and had two children. They were forced by their owners to eat food sacrificed to pagan gods; but when the two children refused and cheerfully put up with the most ferocious tortures under their parents' gaze, Zoe and Hesperus were inspired. Zoe was hung from a tree by her hair and then the whole family were roasted alive for their integrity and faith.

Feast day: 2 May.

A Calendar of Saints

This is a brief index of days and some of the saints commonly associated with them. Calendars differ in the main churches, and have been revised from time to time so some saints may be remembered on different days. This list, however, should give some inspiration for birthdays and namedays.

January

1 Clare of Vienne; William of St Benignus
2 Caspar of Bufalo
3 Genevieve
4 Gregory, Bishop of Langres; Angela of Foligni; Elizabeth Bayley Seton
5 Simeon the Stylite
6 Caspar; Melchior; Balthasar
7 Charles of Sezze; Lucian of Antioch
8 Lucian
9 Adrian of Canterbury; Philip of Moscow
10 Peter Orseolo
11 Theodosius of Antioch
12 Benedict Biscop; Tatiana
13/14 Hilary of Poitiers

14 Felix of Nola, Kentigern (Mungo)
15 Paul the Hermit; Alexander
16 Priscilla; James of Tarentaise; Henry of Northumberland
17 Anthony the Great
18 Margaret of Hungary
19 Henry of Uppsala; Marius and Martha
20 Sebastian
21 Agnes
22 Vincent of Zaragoza; Vincent Pallotti
23 John the Almsgiver; Raymond of Penafort
24 Timothy
25 Paul
26 Paula
27 John Chrysostom; Angela Merici
28 Peter Nolasco
29 François de Sales
30 Martina
31 Aiden of Ferns; John Bosco; Marcella

February

1 Brigid
2 Joan of Lestonnac
3 Lawrence of Canterbury
4 Andrew Corsini; Joan of France; John of Britto; Phileas
5 Agatha
6 Dorothy
7 Theodore the General
8 Cuthman; John of Matha
9 Cyril of Alexandria
10 Clara of Rimini

11 Benedict of Aniane; Victoria
12 Julian the Hospitaller, Marina
13 Katherine of Ricci
14 Valentine
15 Georgia
16 Elias; Gilbert of Sempringham
17 Finan
18 Colman
19 Belina
20 Mildred; Leo the Wonderworker
21 Maurice; George of Amastris
22 Margaret of Cortona
23 Peter Damian; Alexander
24 Matthias
25 Felix III; Robert of Arbrissel
26 Alexander of Egypt; Victor of Arcis-sur-Aube
27 Gabriel Possenti
28 Oswald of Worcester; Angela of Foligno

March

1 David
2 Chad
3 Felix of Africa; Camilla
4 Owen; Adrian
5 Ciaran (Kieran) of Saighir
6 Colette; Felicity
7 Thomas Aquinas
8 Felix of Dunwich; John of God; Julian of Toledo
9 Dominic Savio; Frances of Rome; Gregory of Nyssa; Katherine of Bologna
10 John Sarcander
11 Alberta; Angus

12 Gregory the Great; Maximilian; Paul of Leon;
   Simeon the New Theologian
13 Gerald
14 Matilda
15 Clement; Louise
16 Julian of Antioch; Paul the Simple
17 Gertrude; Joseph of Arimathea; Patrick
18 Edward the Martyr
19 Joseph
20 Herbert; Martin
21 Benedict; Nicholas von Flue
22 Zachary
23 Benedict of Campagna; Fingar
24 Gabriel; Katherine of Vadstena
25 Richard of Paris
26 William of Norwich
27 John the Egyptian; John of Damascus;
   Rupert of Salzburg
28 John of Capestran
29 Mark of Arethusa
30 John Climacus
31 Acacius

April

1 Hugh of Grenoble; Valery
2 Francis of Paola; Mary the Egyptian
3 Richard of Chichester
4 Irene; Benedict the Black
5 Vincent Ferrer; Gerald of Sauve-Majeure
6 William of Aebelholt
7 George of Mitylene; Ursulina
8 Walter; Albert of Vercelli

9 Hugh of Rouen
10 Bede the Younger; Terentius
11 Gemma; Leo I (the Great)
12 Julius; Victor of Braga
13 Justin the Apologist; Winock; Ida
14 Justin
15 Anastasia; Basilissa
16 Benedict Labre; Bernadette; Magnus
17 Robert of Chaise-Dieu; Stephen Harding
18 Eleutherius
19 Leo IX
20 Agnes of Montepuciano
21 Simeon Barsabba'e
22 Conrad
23 George
24 Ivo
25 Mark; William of Monte Vergine
26 Stephen of Perm
27 Peter Canisius; Zita
28 Louis Grignion; Paul of the Cross; Peter Chanel; Valeria
29 Hugh of Cluny; Robert of Molesme
30 Joseph of Cottolengo; Catherine of Siena; Marian and James

May

1 James the Lesser and Philip
2 Anthony of Fiorenze; William of Gellone; Zoe
3 Philip; Alexander I
4 Monica
5 Hilary of Arles; Angelo
6 John Damascene

7 Benedict II; John of Beverley
8 Peter of Tarentaise; Victor
9 Gregory of Nazianzus
10 Francis of Girolamo
11 Walter of Lesterpes
12 Philip of Agyra; Dominic of Calzada
13 Andrew Fournet
14 Michael Garicolts; Mary Mazzarello
15 Dymphna; John-Baptist de la Salle
16 Andrew Bobola; Brendan the Voyager; Simon
   Stock; John of Nepomuk
17 Pascal Baylon
18 Eric; Felix of Cantalice
19 Dunstan
20 Bernardine of Siena
21 Silas of Lucca
22 Rita; Julia of Corsica
23 William of Rochester
24 David of Scotland; Simeon Stylite the Younger;
   Vincent of Lerins
25 Gregory VII; Madeleine Sophie; the Three Marys
26 Mariana of Quito; Philip Neri
27 Julius of Durostorum
28 Bernard of Montjoux; William of Gellone
29 Mary-Magdalene of Pazzi
30 Joan of Arc
31 Petronilla

June

1 Angela of Brescia; Justin
2 Peter and Macellinus
3 Kevin

4 Francis Caracciolo

5 Clement of Volterra; Ferdinand of Portugal

6 Gilbert of Auvergne; Vincent of Umbria

7 Robert of Newminster

8 Melania the Elder; William of York

9 Julian of Edessa; Richard of Andrea

10 Margaret of Scotland; Olivia

11 Barnabas

12 John of Sahagun; Leo III

13 Anthony of Padua

14 Basil the Great

15 Alice; Germaine

16 John Regis

17 Harvey; Emily of Vialar

18 Elizabeth of Schonau; Mark and Marcellian

19 Bruno of Querfurt; Juliana Falconieri

20 Gemma of Saintes

21 Raymond of Belbastri

22 Alban

23 Audrey; Joseph Cafasso

24 John the Baptist

25 Prosper

26 John and Paul

27 Samson; John of Chinon

28 Vincentia Gerosa

29 Peter; Paul

30 Lucina; Peter of Aste; Emma

July

1 Simeon Salus

2 Peter of Luxemburg

3 Aaron and Julius; Leo II

4 Andrew of Crete; Martin of Tours
5 Antony Zaccaria; Philomena of San Severino
6 Maria Goretti
7 Prosper of Aquitaine
8 Elizabeth of Portugal
9 John Fisher; Thomas More; Veronica Giuliani
10 Alexander; Antony of the Caves; Olivia
11 Olga; Oliver Plunket; Benedict
12 John the Iberian; John Gualberto; Veronica
13 Francis Solano; Mildred; Silas; Henry II
14 Vincent of Soignies
15 Edith of Polesworth; Edith of Tamworth;
   James of Nisibus; Swithin
16 Helier; Mary-Magdelen Postel
17 Alexis; Leo IV
18 Arnold; Bruno of Segni; Frederick of Utrecht;
   Marina of Galicia
19 Vincent de Paul
20 Jerome Emiliani; Margaret of Antioch
21 Laurence of Brindisi; Victor of Marseilles
22 Mary Magdalene
23 John Cassian; Bridget of Sweden
24 Christina
25 Christopher; James the Greater
26 Anne; Bartholmea Capitanio
27 Natalia; Clement Slovensky
28 Samson
29 Martha
30 Julitta
31 Helena of Sweden; John Colombino

August

1 Faith
2 Basil the Blessed
3 Peter Eymard
4 Dominic
5 Afra
6 Justus
7 Claudia
8 John-Baptist Vianney; Dominic
9 Oswald
10 Laurence
11 Susanna
12 Clare
13 Irene; John Berchmans
14 Eusebius; Maximilian Kolbe
15 The Blessed Virgin Mary
16 Rock
17 Benedicta; James of York
18 Helen
19 John Eudes; Emily
20 Bernard of Clairvaux
21 Jane Frances de Chantal
22 Timothy of Rome
23 Philip Benizi
24 Bartholomew; Emily de Vialar; Joan Thouret
25 Gregory of Utrecht; Louis IX
26 Elizabeth Bichier des Ages
27 Joseph Calsanz; Monica
28 Julian of Brioude
29 John the Baptist
30 Felix; Rose of Lima
31 Aidan of Lindisfarne; Raymond Nonnatus

September

1 Giles
2 Stephen of Hungary
3 Phoebe; Gregory the Great
4 Hermione; Rose of Viterbo
5 Laurence Giustiniani
6 Bee
7 John of Nicomedia
8 Adrian; Natalia
9 Kieran of Clonmacnois; Isaac the Great; Joseph of
Volokalamsk; Peter Claver
10 Nicholas of Tolentino
11 Felix; Regula; Theodora of Alexandria
12 Guy of Anderlecht
13 Philip of Alexandria; Julian of Ancyra
14 John Chrysostom; Catherine of Genoa
15 Katherine of Genoa
16 Edith of Wilton; Ninian
17 Hildegard; Robert Bellarmine
18 Joseph of Cupertino
19 Emily de Rodat
20 Eustace
21 Matthew
22 Thomas of Villanueva
23 Linus
24 Gerard of Csanad
25 Finbar; Francis of Camporosso; Vincent Strambi
26 Colman
27 Cosmas and Damian; Vincent de Paul
28 Lioba
29 Michael
30 Jerome; Sophia

October

1 Gregory the Enlightener
2 Thomas Cantilupe
3 Gerard of Brogne; Josepha Rossello; Thérèse of
  Lisieux, Thomas of Hereford
4 Francis of Assisi
5 Peregrina; Peter of Imola; Flora of Beaulieu
6 Bruno; Faith
7 Justina
8 Bridget; Margaret
9 Louis Betrand; John Leonardi
10 Daniel; Francis Borgia
11 Alexander Sauli; Bruno; Kenneth (Canice)
12 Wilfrid
13 Edward the Confessor; Gerald of Aurillac
14 Cosmas of Majuma
15 Teresa of Avila
16 Gerard Majella
17 Audrey; Margaret Mary Alacoque
18 Luke
19 John of Rila; Peter of Alcantara
20 Andrew of Crete; John of Kanti
21 John of Bridlington; Ursula
22 Philip of Heraclea
23 Antony Claret
24 Felix of Thibiuca; Raphael
25 Crispin; John of Beverley
26 Evaristus
27 Capitolina and Erotheis
28 Jude; Simon
29 Colman of Kilmacduagh
30 Alphonsus Rodriguez
31 Bee; Quentin

November

1 Harold; Mary of Rome
2 Tobias; George of Vienne; Maura
3 Martin of Porres; Winifred
4 Charles Borromeo
5 Zachary and Elizabeth
6 Leonard
7 Englebert
8 Geoffrey of Amiens
9 Theodore the Recruit
10 Andrew Avellino
11 Bartholomew of Grottaferrata; Martin of Tours
12 Martin I
13 Brice; Frances Cabrini; Nicholas
14 Gregory Palamas; Laurence O'Toole
15 Albert the Great
16 Edmund of Abingdon; Margaret of Scotland
17 Gregory the Wonderworker; Gregory of Tours;
   Hilda; Hugh of Lincoln; Victoria
18 Wynnen; Odo
19 Elizabeth of Hungary
20 Edmund; Felix of Valois
21 Rufus; Albert of Liège
22 Cecilia
23 Alexander Nevsky; Clement; Felicity
24 Flora and Mary; John of the Cross
25 Catherine of Alexandria
26 John Berchmans; Peter of Alexandria
27 Gregory of Sinai
28 James of the March; Stephen the Younger
29 Blessed Cuthbert Mayne
30 Andrew

December

1 Natalia
2 Viviana
3 Francis Xavier
4 Barbara; Peter Chrysologus
5 Crispina
6 Nicholas
7 Martin of Saintes
8 The Blessed Virgin Mary
9 Peter Fourier
10 Eulalia and Julia
11 Daniel the Stylite
12 Finnian of Clonard
13 Lucy
14 John of the Cross
15 Maria di Rosa
16 Adelaide
17 Sturm
18 Rufus and Zosimus; Flannan of Killaloe
19 Blessed Urban V
20 Dominic of Silos
21 Thomas
22 Zeno of Nicomedia; Felix II
23 Victoria of Rome; Ivo of Chartres
24 Anastasia
25 Albert Chmielkowski
26 Stephen
27 Fabiola; John the Apostle
28 Anthony of Lérins
29 Thomas à Becket
30 Anysia; Margaret Colonna; Sebastian Walfré
31 Melania the Younger; Sylvester; John Francis Regis

Index of Names